CHRISTIANITY
THE ORIGINS OF A
PAGAN RELIGION

CHRISTIANITY:
THE ORIGINS OF A
PAGAN RELIGION

Philippe Walter

Translated by Jon E. Graham

Inner Traditions
Rochester, Vermont

Inner Traditions
One Park Street
Rochester, Vermont 05767
www.InnerTraditions.com

Originally published in French under the title *Mythologie chrétienne:
Fêtes, rites et mythes du Moyen Âge* by Éditions Imago, S.A., Paris
First U.S. edition published in 2006 by Inner Traditions

Library of Congress Cataloging-in-Publication Data
Walter, Philippe, 1952–
  [Mythologie chrétienne. English]
  Christianity : the origins of a pagan religion / Philippe Walter ; translated by
Jon E. Graham.— 1st U.S. ed.
      p. cm.
  Includes index.
  ISBN-10: 1-59477-096-4 (pbk.)
  ISBN-13: 978-1-59477-096-8 (pbk.)
  1. Rites and ceremonies—History. 2. Church history—Middle Ages, 600–1500.
  3. Fasts and feasts—History. 4. Mythology—History. I. Title.
  BV35.W3513 2006
  263'.90940902—dc22
                                                          2006008095

Printed and bound in the United States by Lake Book Manufacturing, Inc.

10 9 8 7 6 5 4 3 2 1

Text design and layout by Priscilla Baker and Rachel Goldenberg
This book was typeset in Sabon with Caslon Antique as the display typeface

Inner Traditions wishes to express its appreciation for assistance given by the
government of France through the National Book Office of the Ministère de
la Culture in the preparation of this translation.

Nous tenons à exprimer nos plus vifs remerciements au government de la France
et le ministère de la Culture, Centre National du Livre, pour leur concours dans
le préparation de la traduction de cet ouvrage.

Contents

Introduction

C ould there be a mythology unique to medieval France and Europe? *A priori* we would be tempted to respond in the negative. What among the scattered beliefs and superstitions of the Middle Ages might we compare to the dense network of antiquity that forms a long recognized, perfectly homogenous mythology? What great figure of this alleged medieval mythology could compare with figures such as Zeus and Dionysus?

Yet on closer examination, it does appear that a typically medieval "mythology" has been clearly constructed on top of pagan beliefs that Christianity was forced to incorporate in the interest of keeping such beliefs under its control. Furthermore, if there is a phenomenon that accompanies the development of medieval civilization and coincides with it, it is certainly the flowering of Christianity. Does the combination of the two phenomena count as a Christian mythology in the Middle Ages?

A Christian Mythology

We do not ask here whether Christianity is itself a mythology, but rather how to define the pre-Christian mythological contexts—completely foreign to the Bible—into which Christianity was inserted and which Christianity put to work on its own behalf. There is, in fact, on the periphery of biblical Christianity, an archaic memory of traditions, superstitions,

1

and legends that forms an authentic mythology and possess no biblical justification. During the Middle Ages these rites and beliefs constituted the natural language of a people who did not read the Bible and together provided a context for thinking about the world and the sacred. The essential portion of this mythic material comes out of the "wild" memory of European peoples and, thanks to the Church, was incorporated into the spirit and letter of the Bible. This was how an authentic Christian mythology was manufactured within medieval Christianity (which did not consider itself a mythology).

This Christian mythology of the Middle Ages presents itself first and foremost as a Christianized mythology, for if there is one point on which all religious historians agree, after many useless quarrels, it is the obvious fact that Christianity was not invented on its own in the West and that it was not constructed out of whole cloth. This imported religion was compelled to inscribe its doctrine and commemorations in the pagan calendar predating its arrival in order to better assimilate these preexisting beliefs. The result was an authentic religious compromise in which the part held by the Christian orthodoxy and that held by apocryphal traditions are not easily clarified. The sixteenth-century Reformation restored order to the Christian dogma and eliminated what it considered suspect, including the worship of the Virgin and the saints—precisely where the Christian mythology of the Middle Ages took shelter, which is to say in those practices and beliefs that were not a product of the Bible yet had become part of the Christian faith.

It might be said that it is always easy to smell the myth in a place where it is difficult to verify its presence. Yet there are perfectly explicit testimonies from indisputable medieval authorities explaining the slow process of conquest that Christianity was forced to develop in a region of the world to which it had no prior claim. One such account is a letter from Pope Gregory the Great, by way of Abbot Miletius, to Saint Augustine of Canterbury, who was spreading the gospel among the Angles of England at the beginning of the eighth century.[1] This correspondence clearly explains the policy the Church had established for converting peoples to Christianity:

We wish you to inform him that we have been giving careful thought to the affairs of the English and have come to the conclusion that the temples of the idols among that people should on no account be destroyed. The idols are to be destroyed, but the temples themselves are to be aspersed with holy water, altars set up in them, and relics deposited there. For if these temples are well-built, they must be purified from the worship of demons and dedicated to the service of the true God. In this way, we hope that the people, seeing that their temples are not destroyed, may abandon their error and, flocking more readily to their accustomed resorts, may come to know and adore the true God. And because they have a custom of sacrificing many oxen to demons, let some other solemnity be substituted in its place, such as a day of dedication or the festivals of the holy martyrs whose relics are enshrined there. On such occasions they might well construct shelters of boughs for themselves around the churches that were once temples, and celebrate the solemnity with devout feasting.[2]

This admirable text underscores the persistence of ancient pagan rites and myths during the eighth century and provides one testimony (among many) of the beliefs and customs that the medieval literature of the twelfth or thirteenth century continued to peddle, either candidly or skeptically but with touching insistence. Long ignored or poorly understood, these pagan traces in medieval literature are now available to religious historians and reveal all their mythological importance for a renewed understanding of the culture of the Middle Ages. It remains difficult to define the word *myth*. The three functions that are traditionally acknowledged as part of it—its narrative function (the myth retold), its initiatory function (the myth revealed), and its etiological function (the myth explained)—do not make up a working definition for everyone. This is why it is important to consider the rites that support a myth and extend its life into memory.

Through its relationship to rite, we define *myth* as "the language of a civilization" that inscribes itself into the two fundamental contexts of time and space. In the Christian West, a myth is inseparable from a sacred time and space even if Christianity carries out some revealing transfers in this regard. Thus the Christian Church rearranges in its specific space the three principal elements of druidic worship: the megalithic stone (menhir or dolmen) is transformed into a stone altar; the baptismal font represents the ancient sacred fountain; and the very trees of the forest are transformed into the pillars and columns of a stone nave, with their ornaments of leafy capitals.

Furthermore, if we look at the mythic time inscribed within the ritual calendar, it is clear that a great festival dominated medieval society: Carnival, whose profane liturgies survived the slow erosion of Christianity. The word *carnival* today contains largely depreciated ideas that are merely manifestations of unimportant folklore that has been abandoned to a personal or collective fantasy. Yet the historical and literary study of medieval festivals makes it possible to understand that Carnival goes back to an ancient and venerable time (at least in the Celtic and Indo-European memory). If we know this, its originality is less easily dissolved in the mists of dubious "folklore." Today, Carnival has become a noisy and crazy parentheses in the middle of winter, a means to amuse tourists and provide work for travel agencies. But before it became a collection of amusements and entertainments integrated into our consumer society, Carnival was a religion—it was even *the* religion preceding Christianity and containing an entirely coherent explanation of the world and humans. Capturing the sacred in an original way, it defined the relationships between humans and the Beyond. The Carnival mythology therefore forms the essential framework of medieval mythology.

In order to understand Carnival, it is important to look closely its name and the time and place of its manifestations—in other words, its rites as well as its myths.

The Mythological Calendar of the Middle Ages

We must remember that a mythology is generally inscribed within a calendar that gives rhythm to sacred commemorations and celebrations. Medieval mythology obviously is no exception to this rule, especially if we consider its tight interweaving within Carnival mythology. The

Christian liturgical calendar did not achieve its full effectiveness until the Council of Nicaea established that the Easter commemoration takes into account lunar rhythms and the spring equinox. This made it possible to prop up Christian time with the religious time of European paganism. The period encompassing Carnival, Lent, and Easter forms the true heart of the religious plan of attack of the Middle Ages and offers a time frame in which it is still possible to clearly analyze Christianity's infiltration into paganism and vice versa.

Carnival belongs to a measured and predetermined time, falling under the heading of what Mircea Eliade calls the Great Time—that is, foundational time, the time of origins that witnessed the emergence of myths and cosmogonies. Contrary to a fairly widespread idea, Carnival cannot be reduced merely to the period preceding Lent—that is, the period comprising the time separating Christmas from Ash Wednesday, as it is generally depicted in dictionaries. (For example, the Godefroy* explicitly states under the entry *Carnival:* "the period intended for amusements extending from the day of the Three Kings [Twelfth Night] to Ash Wednesday.") During the year in the Middle Ages there were in fact several carnival periods whose beginnings or ends were celebrated more intensely or specifically. The calendar principle, or devision of the year into eight feast cycles, must be taken into account if we want to grasp the system of rites and myths that overlay Carnival and serve as a framework of the whole of medieval mythology.

The French folklore specialist Claude Gaignebet deduced the internal law of Carnival time: "The road to understanding Carnival is opened precisely through the carving of time into slices of forty days that include the dates of Carnival."[3] From this perspective, the great dates of the Carnival calendar are:

- All Saints' Day (November 1) and Saint Martin's Day
  (November 11)

---

*[The Godefroy refers to Godefroy's *Dictionary of Ninth- to Fifteenth-Century French,* published from 1884 to 1902. —*Trans.*]

- The Twelve Days of Christmas (December 25–January 6)
- Candlemas, Saint Blaise's Day (February 3), Mardi Gras
- Easter (a movable holy day during the period of March 22–April 25)
- Ascension (and the May holidays that occur forty days after Easter)
- Saint John's Day of Summer (June 24)
- Saint Peter's Chains Day (August 1)
- Saint Michael's Day (September 29)

Here we will carefully examine each of these periods, noting the medieval rites, commemorations, and myths connected to them and especially emphasizing the interdependence of the rites and myths assigned to these sacred forty-day periods of the calendar. Looking closely at some of the great figures of male and female saints celebrated on these occasions and their comparison to Celtic models makes it possible to understand not only the continuity but also the metamorphosis of the pre-Christian heritage in medieval Christianity.

Using the works of Pierre Saintyves and Claude Gaignebet as a basis, it becomes clear that a naive reading of medieval hagiography is no longer possible. It becomes unthinkable to take literally such acounts of saints' lives after we have read the profane literature (especially the romances and epics) of the same era. In both genres there appear the same motifs, the same narrative sequences, and sometimes even the same names. The *Legenda Aurea* (Golden Legend)* clearly holds the status of a legendary text and it is folly to read it as a historical document.

It is futile to argue whether the lives of the saints served as the source for the profane literature of the age or the profane writings served as the source for the hagiographic tradition. Instead, we must assume the existence of a mythic imaginal realm that was exploited in two different

---

*The *Legenda Aurea*, or *The Golden Legend*, an account of the lives of a great many saints, was compiled by Jacobus de Voragine in 1260 and became the best-known and most printed medieval hagiography.

ways—in literature and in hagiography. On the one hand, there are too many convergences between these two traditions (the literary and hagiographical) to assume these encounters were the work of chance. On the other hand, there are too many divergences between them to conclude that either tradition was the direct imitation of the other. Thus we must form a third hypothesis: They both derive from the same cultural collection extending to a far older, pre-Christian time—Celtic, at the least. In other words, *The Golden Legend* offers an astonishing sedimentation of pre-Christian mythical, particulary Celtic, motifs that we are able to analyze. As a result, perhaps, there will emerge again the hidden dimensions of a little-known Christian mythology, which, through our perception of it, has the power to profoundly alter our concept of the medieval imaginal realm and oblige us to revisit certain rationales that we have commonly applied to so many medieval texts.

The Mythological Sources of the Middle Ages

What sources do we have at our disposal today for reconstructing the Christian mythology of the Middle Ages? We can note from the start that because testimonies about medieval mythology are never direct, the sources used by modern critical analysis for this reconstruction in no way represent the origin of the traditions peddled by the medieval authors themselves. On the other hand, there is no lack of Latin texts among the antique mythology that was passed on to those in the Middle Ages by means of books and scriptures. The names of the planets, months, or days of the week, for example, necessitate the preservation of the ancient traditions related to Mars (whose name can be found in the French name for Tuesday, *mardi*), Mercury (*mercredi,* or Wednesday), or Jupiter (*jeudi,* Thursday). However, the autochthonous myths (those that did not derive from ancient Greek or Roman culture) were not the object of systematic inventory by medieval scholars because they were in no way considered historical. Furthermore, they were incorporated into a material (literary, historical, or other) that contributed greatly to their concealment.

For those minds fascinated by the marvelous—for writers such as Chrétien de Troyes and early "folklore specialists" such as Gervase of Tilbury, a thirteenth-century collector of stories[4]—this legendary tradition transmitted by word-of-mouth became the working material for art or amusement. For the ecclesiastics educated in the spirit and the letter of the Bible, it instead smacked of aberrations or superstitions that must be fought. Consequently, the less traditional myths were talked about, the better. Yet these myths bequeathed by memory are not illusory. They certainly exist, but they were adulterated in deference to the ecclesiastical need to marginalize the pagan sacrality they evoked. Although they were deformed by Christianity, they did not disappear. The problem such myths pose to people of the modern age therefore concerns less their consistency than how they are read. Documents do exist on medieval mythology, but for the most part, people do not know how to recognize or read them.

It is first necessary to draw up an inventory of the sources capable of providing precise information on the relationship among certain rites, myths, and dates. The correlation becomes quite striking when we realize that these old rites are still practiced today in the modern forms of Carnival. In this way, we can discern an unbroken chain of rites extending from the first written attestations of them to their latest manifestations in modern carnivals. As rite is often better preserved than myth, we look to it to rediscover the spirit of the myths it accompanies.

The written testimonies at our disposal today are primarily (though not exclusively) ecclesiastical documents. It is important to take into consideration this origin in evaluating both their partial presentation of the facts and those details about which they remain silent.

The Acts of Councils

The acts of councils offer a gold mine of testimony that is extremely valuable in helping us pinpoint various rites in relation to calendar feast days. This is how we are able to name the dates connected to the foreseeable dates of the calendar. The *Indiculus superstitionum et paganiarum* issued by the Council of the Leptines in the eighth century contains only headings without any detailed explanation, but certain meaningful titles make it possible to guess at the existence of pagan rites associated with specific calendar periods.

Title 3 of the *Indiculus* is "De spurcalibus in februario." One scholar who has analyzed this document explains:

In February the Germans celebrated holidays honoring the progress of the sun's ascendancy; it was customary to sacrifice pigs on this occasion. These holidays were called Spurcalia. Even today in Holland and lower Germany the month of February is called Sporkel. Because the Germans set great store on these holidays, missionaries shifted them to the time of Christmas and gave them a Christian meaning. Perhaps our Carnival celebrations are a souvenir of the Spurcalia of antiquity?[5]

We can also note that the sacrifice of a pig constitutes one of the primordial rites of Carnival. It so happens that the pig is associated with Saint Anthony, whose feast day is January 17, on the threshold of February and the Spurcalia.

Other pagan customs mentioned in this document are not dated, but thanks to folkloric testimonies, we can rediscover their ritual dates. Title 26 is "De simulacro de consparsa farina," meaning "idols made with flour dough." A modern historian has explained this more precisely: "On certain days the Germans baked breads depicting their gods; these breads were called *Heidenwecke* ('little breads of the pagans'), a name still used in Westphalia to designate the breads eaten during Carnival. The Christ breads, Saint Martin's crescents, the Easter wolves, and the breads of Oerhli Sunday, in the Appenzell region, can all be regarded as souvenirs of this ancient Germanic custom." We can no doubt add to this list our doughnuts (*beignets* or *bugnes*) of Carnival. In fact, the subject of the bread and pastry of Carnival offers a barely explored field of study with the potential for many discoveries.

At times, the ritual dates of the pagan customs mentioned in the

Indiculus or in other, similar texts are not indicated, but it is not at all difficult to determine what they may have been. For instance, Saint Gregory's letter to Saint Augustine of Canterbury states explicitly that certain cattle sacrifices took place at precise dates of the year in the proximity of certain saints' days. The allusion to the sacrifice of cattle brings to mind the custom of killing the fatted cow that is often practiced during Carnival. Gérard de Nerval mentions it as still occurring in the nineteenth century.[6] In Paris since at least the fifteenth century, a fatted cow was paraded through the streets by a joyful procession of butchers. It seems the butchers guild had obtained an ordinance giving them the exclusive privilege of this parade. The custom was already at this time nothing more than a simple amusement, but it probably recalls ancient rites that placed the cow at the heart of very old religious mysteries. In fact, the importance of bovines can be found at the heart of old Indo-Iranian rites and in the Hindu worship of sacred cows.

The letter of Pope Gregory written at the beginning of the eighth century also mentions cabins made of branches that were erected under certain circumstances. These probably refer to the "leaf-covered" bowers mentioned randomly in several medieval texts, such as the *Jeu de la Feuillée* (The Play of the Bower) and which belong to the customs of May.

The Penitentials

Along with testimony provided by the acts of the councils, we can find evidence of possible pagan rites in the penitentials, or confessors' manuals, containing the questions to ask the faithful during confession. These books indicate the "tariff" of penitence that is to be assessed to the sinners. For our purpose, they also contain references to certain rites associated with precise dates of the year—rites that were generally practiced during the major dates of Carnival.

For example, chapter 62 of the *Penitential* of Burchard, the bishop of Worms (965–1025), mentions several pagan rites associated with January 1:

Have you celebrated the calends* of January according to pagan customs? Have you undertaken an exceptional or uncommon task on the occasion of the new year, a task that you work on neither before or after—to wit: arranging stones on your table or giving a feast, leading dancers and singers through the streets and squares, taking a seat upon your roof while wearing your sword in order to see and know what will happen to you in the new year, sitting atop a bull's hide where the roads cross to read the future, on the night of January 1 cooking bread for yourself to know whether the new year will be prosperous depending on whether the dough rises? If yes, because you have abandoned God your creator, and have turned to vain idols and become apostate, you will fast on all the official days for two years.

And chapter 104 offers this: "Have you done like some during the calends of January, the eighth day of the Nativity? During this holy night, they spin, weave, sew, begin all manner of works—at the instigation of the devil—on the occasion of the new year. If yes, [you must] fast forty days on bread and water."[7]

Les Dits de saint Pirmin (The Sayings of Saint Pirmin), of the eighth century, formulated a number of prohibitions relating to calendar feast days that were themselves borrowed from even older texts: "What could it be if not demoniacal worship to celebrate the Vulcanales and the calends . . . You, men, adorn yourselves not in the clothing of women, nor you, women, in the garb of men, on the occasion of the calends or of certain holidays."[8]

There is no need to emphasize the carnivalesque aspect of the disguise referred to here that plays on gender reversal. Even today, in Belgium on Fat Sunday cross-dressing men—the Mam'zèles—prepare for the great parade on Fat Tuesday. These men disguised as women bring

---

*[The *calends* refers to the first day of the month, according to the ancient Roman calendar. Originally it designated the first day of the new moon. From it days were counted backward to determine the *ides*. —*Trans*.]

to mind the cross-dressing that appears in certain Dionysian ceremonies in Greece. Mircea Eliade has analyzed the rite of disguising from the perspective of the androgyne:

> If we take into account that transvestitism was very widespread during Carnival and the spring festivals of Europe and also in various agricultural ceremonies in India, Persia, and other Asian countries, we can grasp the principal function of this rite. In short, it involves one's emergence from oneself, the transcendence of one's personal, strongly historicized status and the recovery of one's original status, which was transhuman and transhistorical, preceding the formation of human society.[9]

With his mention of the Vulcanales, was Saint Pirmin alluding to the festivals of August 23, which, in ancient Rome, were intended to prevent fires, or was he using this term to designate other festivals that he might have witnessed that were reminiscent of the Vulcanales? The latter conclusion is probably more accurate. Ritual fires were lit on this date to tame the god Vulcan. The Latin grammarian Varron gives us an explanation for this: "The Volcanalia take their name from Vulcan, whom they celebrate. On this day, to redeem themselves the people hurl animated figures into the fire . . ."[10]

Such a custom obviously brings to mind the fires of Saint John, which could have been confused for those that were lit in honor of Vulcan. An educated man might make this scholarly comparison, confusing two traditions that were foreign to each other in order to explain the supposed origin of a profane custom, and then rejecting them both with the same condemnation. In fact, the fires of Saint John do not derive directly from the Volcanalia, but instead are quite likely an analogous expression of myths and rites that go back to a common Indo-European origin. Vulcan was the smith god confused with Hephaistos. It so happens that the day after Saint John's of Summer is the celebration dedicted to Saint Eloi, a Christianized figure who is an offshoot of the ancient smith god of the Celts. This explains the intentional (or unintentional) confusion of Varron.

What we discern here, however, is the principal obstacle on which stumble all historians of religions: finding in Roman antiquity the origin of a given medieval custom when, in fact, both customs are independent of each other and instead hark back to a common (Indo-European) origin. From this point of view, it is perfectly false to say that the medieval festival of the fools refers back to the Saturnalia of antiquity. It is more reasonable to assert that the medieval festival of the fools and the Saturnalia both reach back to an even older common mythological blueprint that explains some of their components.

Profane Literary Texts

Not only religious texts help us to understand the roots of medieval myths; profane literary texts also improve our understanding of the medieval Carnival rites. Arthurian romances and chansons de geste are bathed in myth. The sources of these products of the imaginal realm can be sought in an archaic past because it is common and fully accepted knowledge that the period of the Middle Ages was not successful at inventing its stories. It drew them from an old, rich oral tradition and a very vibrant folklore.

The fictional literature of the Middle Ages contains a number of testimonies on the calendar festivals and the great figures who dominated the medieval imagination. I have devoted a study of them to the period 1170–1235. This inventory, limited to France, brings to light numerous representations of profane ceremonies connected to the cycle of Carnival.[11] For the most part, such representations can be found again in post-medieval folklore, embedded in the festivals of May, the customs of Saint John's Day, and the rites of Mardi Gras.

Unfortunately, the Latin literature of the Middle Ages is still poorly explored even to this day. There is a great abundance of it extending from long before the twelfth century to the junction of late antiquity and the Middle Ages. It holds a large number of valuable secrets that we still are not quite equipped to grasp. Several rare documents cannot fail to intrigue the folklore scholar and the mythologist, defying as they do traditional explanations based on rationalism or assumptions of the lack of value of these testimonies.

A satiric eleventh-century text by the archbishop Adalberon of Laon presents a monk who disguises himself as a blacksmith or farrier on the first day of December. This unusual disguise is very easily explained if we realize that December 1 is the commemoration of Saint Eloi, the goldsmith and blacksmith of King Dagobert. It so happens that in the hagiographic system, this figure is the Christianized version of an old Celtic deity of the forge no doubt comparable to the Celtic Gobinu. In the archbishop's narrative, the monk must disguise himself again "before March 1"—in other words, during a period that corresponds exactly to the time of Carnival.

The magician blacksmith is a key figure in the myths of Carnival. The disguise of the monk is part of Carnival's satire, but it also demonstrates that medieval authors had specific intentions (literary or polemical) when they incorporated certain features borrowed from the ethnographical reality of the holidays of their time. The echoes of these holidays are necessarily altered by a literary rewrite, but they are perfectly recognizable to anyone who has even a slight familiarity with relatively contemporary Carnival liturgies and folklore.

The medieval chronicles in Latin offer a quantity of facts that the authors sometimes relate to a ritual date with mythical value. In the Norman chronicle of the eleventh century, there is, for example, the encounter with the Mesnie Hellequin,* a parade of revenants led by a sinister, club-wielding figure behind whom is concealed a major deity of the Otherworld. This procession is very precisely placed on the night of December 31 into January 1, during the calends of January, which are well known for their superstitions. In fact, the Norman chronicle, written by Orderic Vital, blends remnants of legend with the evocation of an authentic fear of the night. It underscores the permanent nature of legendary traditions that easily incorporate actual events to craft a mix that is both poetic and historical and emphasizes the mythical components.

---

*[The Mesnie Hellequin is the French term for the Wild Hunt. —*Trans.*]

This text forms a document of the utmost importance regarding medieval mythology, and we must give it a noteworthy place in our study.

The historiographical work of Gregory of Tours, which is even older than that of Orderic Vital, gains from being studied from both a mythological and a historical perspective. Though Herodotus had already conceived a chronicle similar in nature, it succeeds in relating, in spite of itself, a mass of legendary deeds that historians have often taken for real ones. A comparative study of the episodes within Gregory's narrative illustrates the very composite nature of medieval chronicles, which are nourished by an ancient fund of legends, beliefs, and superstitions at the same time that they claim to depict specific historical events. Such chronicles can make a large contribution to the understanding of the mythological universe of the early Middle Ages, given that medieval myth and folklore are intertwined in the honeycomb vaults of history and literature in unexpected yet decisive ways.

Hagiographic Texts

Hagiographic texts constitute, beyond all shadow of doubt, the richest source of information on the mythology of the Middle Ages. Here we will refer especially to Jacques de Voragine's *The Golden Legend,* which offers a compilation of the principal hagiographic traditions of the thirteenth century.

In reality, the number of hagiographic texts of the time is beyond count, and most are still waiting for a systematic study of their mythological aspects. Medieval hagiography was the machine used for Christianizing the old European myths and represents the most accomplished expression of the Christian mythology of the Middle Ages. As noted by Pierre Saintyves, the hagiographic legends or the passions of the martyrs are often nothing but potpourris of features borrowed from folk tradition. It is important to be aware of this and not to succumb to the illusion of historicity they can engender.

The study of hagiographic legends cannot be led today from a narrow historical or historicizing perspective. It is no longer reasonable to ask if this or that saint actually passed through a particular city of France during some specific year. Medieval hagiography is a literary genre just like others, with its codes and narrative rites, its themes, and its imagery. During the Middle Ages this genre rarely responded to the demands of a historically rigorous logic; instead, it was based on an ideologically and culturally premeditated fabrication as well as on a certain number of rules that are easy to discern once we are no longer duped by the marvels contained in these texts. Many saints were invented to serve the needs of Christianization or were brought into being for economic reasons (including the necessity of attracting pilgrims to a particular sanctuary). Many lives of the saints were manufactured or recopied from earlier models that were equally fictitious.

It is pointless to read these hagiographic legends in the light of history alone. Their imaginary and mythical content has much more to teach us than does their alleged historical testimony. Medieval hagiography can be defined as the Christian reformulation of a certain number of pagan—in other words, pre-Christian (particularly Celtic)—motifs. Following the example of archaeologists, it is necessary to scrub from a hagiographical text its Christian patina in order to find in its depths a certain number of archaic motifs that reflect a kind of "savage thought" that is totally foreign to Christianity. It is no longer possible to read naively or superficially a hagiographic text; such a work necessarily finds its rightful place in a coded system of motifs, a mythological memorandum, that can shed light on both the pagan and the Christian aspects of certain rites and the saints they celebrate.

The hagiographic texts offer several advantages to those who analyze them from the perspective of the marvelous. They have conserved a great deal and sometimes contain details of incredible precision that reveal a great deal about the mind-set—even including a fetishism of words and motifs—of the early Middle Ages. Furthermore, they are inscribed within a historical time frame that is easy to determine (that of the writing or copying of manuscripts in abbeys and ending with the time of Gutenberg) and in a ritual time (the order of the days and the commemorations) that preserves the calendrical context of the pagan myths. From the presence of certain events in the lives of certain saints, it is possible to deduce specific mythological aspects related to the pagan festivals they Christianized, especially when these saints are celebrated in close proximity to a particular date of the pre-Christian (or Carnival) calendar.

As Claude Gaignebet explains so well, not just any saint has succeeded just any pagan figure at just any moment of the year. Hagiographic literature in fact forms a veritable pagan mythological code for which no one has yet truly grasped the key (especially not those specialists in Christian hagiography who still believe that a saint's celebration day is the anniversary of his or her death). It is wrong to say that the myths preceding Christianity were not preserved and that we lack documentation of these myths. To the contrary, there is an abundance of such documentation. Pre-Christian myths have been conserved in pieces in the hagiographic puzzle constructed throughout the Middle Ages. It is simply necessary that we learn how to find and decipher them.

Only a comparative method can aptly extract from hagiographic texts the elements of pagan culture they contain and the authentic mystical thought that governs them. The most illuminating example is certainly that of Saint Blaise, whose feast day is February 3. It just so happens that this day is precisely the one Rabelais recognized as the date of Gargantua's birth. Claude Gaignebet gives us a perfect analysis of the worship of Saint Blaise.[12] It was said that this bishop and saint of Armenia saved from death a child who was choking on a fish bone and that he had the ability to talk to wild animals, who could understand him. Throughout the Middle Ages, Saint Blaise remained the protector against throat ailments. Thus was born on February 3 Gargantua, son of Grandgousier and Gargamelle, hero of the throat,* of great feasting in the style of Carnival, and of the inspired word. Blaise is also reminiscent of the figure of Master Blaise, the well-known scribe of Merlin in the Arthurian romances.

---

*[*Grandgousier* translates as "big gullet" or "big throat." The name Gargamelle, mother of Gargantua, is another French slang word for "gullet." —*Trans.*]

Medieval Iconography

Another rich source for our investigation is medieval iconography (manuscripts, the capitals of Romanesque churches, and so on), which constitutes a fairly neglected secondary area for the understanding of medieval Carnival rites. The interpretation of iconographic documents is often a delicate matter that has at times provided an opportunity for excess. Virtually any significance could be ascribed to an unexpected detail or some incongruous feature of a saint. Haven't people gone so far as to invent traditions and imagine remote or decidedly exotic precursors for details that have a much simpler explanation in the reality of autochthonous myths and in the immediate Celtic, if not pre-Celtic, past?

Once the sources of medieval Christian practices have been identified and studied, we must organize the results of a comparative investigation within an explanatory context that will not overly alter the source we have uncovered. In fact, if a living mythology existed in the Middle Ages, it was celebrated in rites and festivals. It is not possible to separate rite from myth. Thus, in order to avoid all artificial theoretical constructions, it is preferable to adopt a calendrical or chronological inventory, rather than an alphabetical inventory of rites and myths, despite the recurrence of the same rites on different dates. In several studies preceding mine here, there have been identified in European folklore the remnants of ritual practices that are more or less scattered and often misunderstood. There was then an attempt, using the aid of medieval texts, to demonstrate the logic and buried continuity of these practices. Little by little, a mental architecture took shape that was just as revealing in any understanding of medieval literature as it was in comprehending the folklore that came from the same memory.

This work claims to be only the beginning of a vaster and more systematic research. Rather than being an exhaustive study, it merely lays the framework for studies yet to come. What it attempts primarily, based on a few specific examples, is to put into perspective certain hagiographic conundrums that have been unfairly evaluated until now. It seeks to challenge the usual reading of these texts that has led to false certainties . . . or to uncertainties that are, in fact, true.

ONE

Carnival, the Enigma of a Name

Near the door to the room, Pantagruel spotted
Gargantua's little dog, which he named Kyne.
RABELAIS, *GARGANTUA AND PANTAGRUEL*, 3.35

S crutinizing a myth requires scrutinizing the names it carries. Even today, the word *carnival* is an enigma to philologists. Regardless of the etymological dictionary we consult, the entry is perplexing, leading to either annoying uncertainty or dubious acknowledgment. Uncertain etymology, artificial explanations, and belated verifications make up the fog surrounding the word *carnival* and reveal a certain lexicology that is ignorant of both anthropology and the history of religions. Can we write a history of words if we are ignorant of the history of that to which these words refer? Yet this is what seems to have occurred with the word *carnival*.

The Uncertainty of Dictionaries

The very recent and monumental *Trésor de la langue française* (Treasury of the French Language) sums up the current consensus of etymological science on the word *carnival*:

Borrowed from the Italian *carnevalo* (-le) confirmed in the thirteenth century, a modification perhaps encouraged by the Latin

19

Natale, "Christmas." From the medieval Latin *carnelevare* (965 in the Latium), clearly attested in northern Italy during the twelfth century, consisting of *carne,* "meat," and *levare,* either in the sense of "taking off" (cf. the concurrent type in Italy, *carne laxare*) or in the sense provided by the amusing alteration of the phrase *jejunium levare,* "maintain a fast," or *jejunium levare de carne,* "to abstain from meat." The 1268 attestation could be due to a local relationship with Tuscan merchants (cf. FEW, vol. 2, 391b). The primary meaning would thus be "[entrance into] Lent," then "eve of the entrance into Lent" through a semantic evolution parallel to that of *carême prenant.* *

Despite a convincing appearance, this definition is ultimately highly unsatisfying and offers at least two points that are open for discussion, both related to the Christian interpretation of Carnival, which the definition simply repeats from medieval authors.

The first objection is based on linguistics: the relationship between *carnevalo* and *carnelevare* is debatable and philologically uncertain. On this point it is appropriate to draw a distinction between the scientific etymology and the medieval etymology. The relation between the words *carnevalo* and *carnelevare* is in fact derived from an etymological device of rhetoric treatises and is closer to wordplay than to relationship of true linguistic derivation.

The second point of objection is anthropological: The etymology of the word by way of *carne levare* is not acceptable because the word *carnival* designates not only Ash Wednesday, the time when meat is "taken away" (*carne levare*), as the definition's interpretation suggests, nor the period when it is necessary to say "good-bye" (*vale* in Latin) to meat (*carnevale*). In fact, as the majority of contemporary dictionaries indicate, Carnival designates the period of amusements that extends from the Day of the Kings (Epiphany) to Ash Wednesday. Yet this defi-

---

*[Carême Prenant refers to the three days of celebration preceding Ash Wednesday. — *Trans.*]

nition of Carnival is still too restrictive, for there are several Carnival-like periods during the year, providing one more reason to abandon the etymological play on *carne levare*. Is it somewhat paradoxical to name as "the moment when meat is taken away" (*carne levare*) those other Carnival-like periods during year when meat is eaten in large quantities? Furthermore, if we follow the above definition's etymological explanation, every Friday on which Christians are forbidden to eat meat would be a day of Carnival, which is obviously not the case. It is therefore necessary to find other basis for an etymological discussion of the term.

The Word *Carnival* during the Middle Ages

In support of the definition in the *Trésor de la langue française,* we can look to the existence during the Middle Ages of a word such as *carnelevale,* first appearing in a Milanese *ordo* (liturgy manual) of 1130, or of the word *carnelevamine,* appearing in an 1195 charter. Such words, however, only encourage more confusion. *Carneval, carnelevamine,* and *carnelevale* seem interchangeable: These terms all designate the same reality in three slightly different forms. Given the standardized use of Latin by the Church, why would such variations of form exist? Could they represent dialect-based nuances, or were there truly several names for Carnival?

When using the various forms of the word cited above, the medieval clerics were in fact playing on the word *carnival* in order to extract its presumed etymology. Modern etymologists have succumbed to the same pseudo-etymological gloss of the word already attested to in the Middle Ages. We know that during this period, wordplay was quite common, not for the purposes of humor or irony, but for hermeneutic ends.[1] It was necessary to make words and names speak in a way that would bring out a meaning to conform to the teachings of the Church. Isidore of Seville left us a book of etymology that is quite enlightening regarding the way words were triturated during the Middle Ages to make them say what someone wanted them to say:

> Etymology is the origin of words when the elements that make up the meaning of a verb or a noun are united by means of an explanation. Aristotle called it symbol, while Cicero called it annotation because it makes known (*nota*) the meaning of the nouns and verbs that represent the real world by acting as its referents. For example, *flumen* (river) comes from *fluendo* (to flow) because it was created by flowing.[2]

This conception of etymology makes possible every delirious interpretation, and the word *carnival* has suffered all the hazards of this curious method of Medieval elucidation. Etymology *per syllabus*—that is, dividing words into syllables, as in a rebus—played the role of linguistic explanation during the Middle Ages. Here is the origin of the uncertainty and the phenomenon of pseudo-etymology surrounding the word *carnival* glossed into *carnelevale* (or *carniprivium*, as corroborated by Gervase of Tilbury in the thirteenth century). Each syllable is said to signify something in reference to an existing homonym in the language of the time. This etymological tinkering would certainly allow the word a Christian explanation that conforms with Church doctrine.

While the word *carnival* appears in several forms with various endings, it always begins with the same root: *carn(e)*. This seems to indicate that the clerics reinterpreted the end of the word they were using, either because they could not identify it (which made it necessary to make known the unknown by replacing the end of the word with other terms that were clearer and more familiar to them) or because they were seeking to camouflage a taboo word that called to mind overly impious realities that were unacceptable to the Christian faith. *Carnival* could thus have been Christianized into *carne levare*, which attaches the meaning "taking away meat" to aide the Church in justifying Lent in the face of pagan rites and beliefs. In a sense, it was trying to eliminate Carnival by giving it the meaning of Lent. Originally, however, the two periods were perfectly distinct and even diametrically opposed; thus, our confusion surrounding this term is perfectly justified. It is significant that the manipulated forms of the word *carnival* can be found in clerical texts or those written by ecclesiastics.

One more interesting aspect to the word's alteration lies in the fact that behind this linguistic tinkering there lies a form of superstition that is typical of primitive mentalities. To name a deity (and Carnival would then have been a deity) could be dangerous because it amounted to giving him a potentially harmful power over humans and the world. Conversely, disguising the deity's name rendered it inoffensive and permitted its use in any context. The memory and the tradition to which this name refers are therefore further muddied.

One thing is certain: We can find no corroboration of the word *carnival* in French before 1268. It should be noted, however, that this absence of any written corroboration does not mean the word or one like it did not exist in the oral tradition.[3]

Godefroy's dictionary cites a 1268 text from the Bouillon region that mentions the *nuyct de quarnivalle*. This is the first French appearance of the word in a written form that might awaken Italian consonance. Must we turn toward Italy, then, to understand the origin of the word? This is actually a very viable notion if we take into consideration the testimonies concerning an ancient Italic deity predating Christianity: the goddess Carna.

Carna: The Goddess of Pork and Beans

Carna and *carnival:* We can immediately note the resemblance of the two words. Of course, this outer resemblance does not prove a direct derivation of the latter term from the name Carna or that scholars of the medieval West borrowed from an ancient text. An Indo-European root related to *carna* and common to *carnival* and *carna* could have served as a link in this evolution. The Indo-European kinship must be retained here, at least as a hypothesis. Yet we can still look to the goddess Carna to find a mythological context related to the word *carnival.*

Who is Carna? Ovid mentions this mythical figure in the *Fasti*. In fact, in general the work of the Latin poet forms a valuable index to the myths and rites of ancient Italy classified according the calendar. He provides clear documentation on the archaic Roman religion as practiced in the first six months of the year (for only half of the work has survived).

We know that the goddess Carna was celebrated during the calends of June, a position that signals a particular role of worship and the rites associated with it. (The calends always formed a powerful period of the Roman calendar.)

In Rome on June 1, arbutus branches were hung above the doors and windows to keep away the *stirges,** which were said to gnaw the intestines of nursing babies. In the *Fasti*, Ovid tells how arbutus "drives away from one's doors all misfortunate accident":

> There are some greedy birds, not those that cheated
>> Phineus of his meal, though descended from that race:
>> Their heads are large, their eyes stick out, their beaks
>> Fit for tearing, their feathers are grey, their claws hooked.
>> They fly by night, attacking children with absent nurses,
>> And defiling their bodies, snatched from the cradle.
>> They're said to rend the flesh of infants with their beaks,
>> And their throats are full of the blood they drink.
>> They are called screech owls, and the reason for the name
>> Is the horrible screeching they usually make at night.[4]

Ovid goes on to relate the curse that had befallen Phocas, a male infant five days old. The child is attacked by stirges, who literally tear into him. Drawn by his cries, the nurse demands help. A woman named Cranaë (who is the goddess Carna)[5] offers to heal the child:

> Quickly she touched the doorposts, one after the other,
>> Three times, with Arbutus leaves, three times with Arbutus

---

*[Also *strix* or *striga,* a legendary bird commonly presumed to be modeled on the screech owl. —*Trans.*]

Marked the threshold, sprinkled the entrance with water,
Medicinal water, while holding the entrails of a two-month sow
And said: "Birds of night, spare his entrails;
A small victim is offered here for a small child.
Take a heart for a heart, I beg, flesh for flesh,
This life we give you for a dearer life."
When she had sacrificed, she placed the severed flesh
In the open air and forbade those there to look at it.
A rod of Janus, taken from a whitethorn, was set
Where a little window shed light into the room.
After that, they say, the birds avoided the cradle,
And the boy recovered the color he had before.

Macrobius, a writer of late antiquity, contributes some additional information about the worship of Carna:

There are some who believe that the month of June took its name from Junius Brutus, the first Roman consul, because as the expulsion of Tarquin transpired this month (during the calends of June), Brutus would have sacrificed to Carna on the Caelian Hill in fulfillment of an oath. It was believed that Carna ruled over man's vital organs. Consequently, it was she to whom one turned to ask that the liver, the heart, and the viscera of the body in general be kept in good health, and as it was thanks to her heart and the dissimulation she had contrived that Brutus had succeeded in changing an evil reign of government, it was also to this goddess, patron of the vital organs, that he dedicated a temple. One also offers as a sacrifice to Carna a puree of beans and lard, food that contributes more than any other to the body's strength. As ripe beans were used in this month's worship, the calends of June were also vulgarly known as the "calends of the beans."[6]

Among the rites dedicated to Carna, the food offerings are the most notable. As indicated in the above passage from Macrobius, an offering of a puree of beans and lard was given to Carna. Lard, so closely associated with meat, makes it easy to underscore its carnivalesque aspect. Sausages, hams, and other fatty meats have been part of the gastronomy of Carnival for a long time. Carnival is first and foremost a time of heavy eating, an excess of food and "Gargantuan" or Pantagruelian* feasts, and this is true in no matter what realm Carnival takes place. Such a rite seems consistent with the root that most etymologists recognize in Carnival: *caro*, meaning "meat." Furthermore, in old French, the word that predated Carnival was *carnage* (or *charnage*), defined as a ritual meat sacrifice, most likely for a sacred and grandiose feast. The goddess Carna's protection and strengthening of the vital forces was connected to the particular nutritional value attached to certain dishes served in her honor. Ovid seems to confirm this interpretation when describing the ritual:

> You ask why we eat greasy bacon fat on the calends,
> And why we mix beans with parched grain.
> She is an ancient goddess, nourished by familiar food,
> No epicure to seek out alien dainties . . .
> Pigs were prized; men feasted on slaughtered swine:
> The earth yielded only beans and hard grains.
> They say that whoever eats these two foods together
> At the calends, in this sixth month, will have sweet digestion.

But why did the bean hold such a privileged place in the worship of Carna? We can further clarify the connection between the rite and the myth with Ovid's testimony.

The King of the Bean

The myth related to the bean in the Latin world is associated with the Fabii, whose name, appropriately enough, comes from the Latin *faba*, meaning "bean." The Fabii was a brotherhood of young men loyal to

---

*[Like Gargantua, Pantagruel was a giant who figured in Rabelais's book. —*Trans.*]

Remus, the twin brother of Romulus. Its celebration took place during the ides of February, on the thirteenth day of the month, during an eminent carnivalesque period of the year. In his work on Carnival, Claude Gaignebet recalls and describes the exploits of the Fabii, those men of the bean. It should be no surprise to find *carnage* here again and the ritual meal that unites the community of dinner guests:

> During a feast of Faunua, at the time of the twin founders, when all were readying themselves to taste the entrails of a sacrificed goat, thieves made off with their herd of cattle. Without taking the time to get dressed, they set off in pursuit of the cattle. With his Fabii, Remus succeeded in regaining them, and when he returned first to the place of sacrifice, he cried out, "The victors alone shall eat." Arriving too late, Romulus found nothing but gnawed bones and felt remorse that his brother and his brother's men had been more fortunate than he and his Quintalii. The struggle between the two groups of youth, a ritual struggle, ends here with the triumph of the individuals who are the closest to the wild state; those whose antisocial character will subsequently get them expelled from the city.[7]

Ovid places this episode in January. In the eighth book of the *Aenead*, Virgil explores its subsequent development. We should note that since the time of antiquity, the bean has possessed a very rich mythological history. We know that Pythagoras excluded it from his diet because he viewed it as having blood and was consequently an animal, thus a food contrary to his vegetarian diet. Cicero (in *De Divinatione*) thought the bean was impure and that it spoiled the blood, caused the stomach to swell, excited sensuality, and caused bad dreams. The bean, then, could be said to be the Carnival food par excellence, given that it causes the stomach to swell and can therefore make a man resemble a pregnant woman. There are a great number of Carnival brotherhoods that find amusement in the ambiguity brought on by this bloating.

Claude Gaignebet furthermore recalls that, according to the Pythagorean literature, the bean takes forty days to germinate. It therefore follows the exact same interval of Carnival time based on the forty-day period (Lent = forty days before Easter, Ascension = forty days after Easter). It is no cause for surprise, then, that the bean can be found in the rites of Carnival—most particularly, those of Epiphany, for the bean, as we know, appears in the king's cake.* The person who finds the bean becomes, as a joke, the temporary king of the feast within the time of Carnival.

Therefore Carna, goddess of the bean, introduces us to the liturgical mysteries of Carnival even if her feast of June 1 seems not to be part of the Carnival calendar. In reality, as Georges Dumézil shows us, there is a close connection between Carna, the goddess of the calends of June, and Helernus, the god of the calends of February: Carna is the daughter of Helernus, the result of "sowing" on the worship site of Helernus.

> The date of the sacrifice offered to Helernus (calends of February) and, as described by Ovid, the line of descent from Helernus and Carna, goddess who rules over the transformation of food into flesh and whose feast (calends of June) is called Kalendae fabariae, allows us to understand, through reference to agronomists' instructions, the function of this god: For three months he protects the beans and generally the garden plants of spring.[8]

The Italic goddess Carna or her Celtic counterpart obviously does not have a direct reincarnation in medieval Christianity. The theology of Carna was too violently condemned by the Church. Further, following Carnival, the Church imposed Lent and the prohibition of all meat foods as if this periodic dietary taboo would once and for all exorcise this pagan figure as well as the the table customs she encouraged.

This logically leads us to raise the following question: Is there a

---

*[It is customary in Europe, particularly in France, to serve a cake named after the three Magi in which has been cooked a bean or other object. The person who finds the bean in his or her slice is considered to be the beneficiary of good luck for the following year. —*Trans.*].

myth of Carnival that connects all the rites of the period? Folklore scholars such as Arnold van Gennep have always denied the existence of such a myth. Their often limited and superficial knowledge of medieval literature has not allow them to discern that behind certain incongruous literary schemes lurk the pieces of a perfectly coherent mythological system. Again, it is necessary to be able to sense, beneath the literary patina of a medieval text, the structuring system of the myths and rites that were used to organize the narrative content of the work in question. Of course, we must show proof that these myths and rites belong to the time of Carnival and form part of its base—and only a method using comparison offers the possibility of coming up with tangible results. Nothing can be deduced from a single, isolated text, and any story can be misleading. One criterion of comparison whose value is undeniable is that of the calendar rite.

In fact, medieval literature, which often borrowed its material from an older oral tradition, preserved the rites more completely than the myths, no doubt because myths were the raw materials of a stories that, over the course of time, metamorphosed in various adaptations and literary rewrites. These original legends became unrecognizable because they had melted into newer fictional stories that grew from them. Rites, on the other hand, remained relatively fixed in their outer form while sometimes changing in meaning, depending on the contexts in which they appeared.

La Manekine and Carnival

The testimony of a thirteenth-century literary text provides the context of legend that completes the data we have examined thus far. It offers a clear grasp of both a rite and a Carnival date. The text is *La Manekine* (Little Lass), a romance written by Philippe de Remy toward the middle of the thirteenth century.[9] Here is a short synopsis:

A king of Hungary was married to a very pretty woman who had given birth to a superb daughter named Joie. Before the queen died, she made her husband promise that after her death, he would marry a woman like her.

Upon her death, he asked his barons to find him a woman as beautiful as she, but their searches ended in vain. Finally, it became clear that there was but one woman who corresponded to the desire of the king and the dead queen: Joie. The king of Hungary was then advised to wed his own daughter.

After hearing her father's intentions, however, Joie refused outright this marriage against nature. Nevertheless, his decision to marry her was firm and irrevocable—though the king did grant his daughter reprieve until Candlemas. To escape the inevitable abhorred union, Joie cut off her hand and threw it into the river, which prompted her father to condemn her to be burned alive at the stake.

On Candlemas, the seneschal, taken with pity, placed Joie on a rudderless craft and abandoned her to the waves. The drifting boat carried her to Scotland, where, on the Firebrand Sunday (the first Sunday of Lent), she arrived at the house of the king, who welcomed her and immediately named her La Manekine. He fell in love with Joie, despite the hostility of his mother, who was destroyed at seeing her son in love with a cripple. In her desperation, she plotted revenge.

Soon, La Manekine and the king of Scotland were wed and La Manekine became pregnant. Eventually, her time to deliver arrived, but because the king was away in France at a tournament, he could not attend the birth. Wishing to inform her husband of the birth of his son, John, La Manekine sent him a letter, but it was intercepted by the queen mother, who replaced it with another missive announcing that La Manekine had given birth to a monster.

After receiving the letter, the king of Scotland asked his family nonetheless to take care of the mother and "child," but this letter also was intercepted by La Manekine's mother-in-law and was replaced this time by one urging the Scots to burn La Manekine and her son. The time was now the final days of Carnival, approaching Lent.

Devastated by this condemnation, the seneschal replaced La Manekine and her son with two wooden simulacra, which would be burned in their stead while the condemned mother and infant were left to the mercy of the waves in a boat that was said to drift all the way to Rome, where the king and La Manekine were reunited on Palm Sunday. Finally, on Easter Sunday, La Manekine also regained her hand.

Ritual dates from both the popular and liturgical calendars appear throughout this story, which was based on a common folktale. On Candlemas (February 2) the king wishes to marry his daughter. Three days later she is abandoned to the mercy of the waves on a boat that reaches Scotland on Firebrand Sunday. She marries the king of Scotland on Pentecost. Two years later, in January, she gives birth to a son. At the beginning of Lent, the king, who had been away traveling, returns to Scotland, where he learns that a boat holding his wife and son, both saved from the stake, had been left to the mercy of the waves.

One date that we must note in this narrative is Firebrand Sunday (or first Sunday of Lent). This key day of the Carnival calendar is associated with bonfires that hark to those on which, on two occasions, La Manekine was scheduled to be burned. The bonfire also calls to mind the cremation rites that Carnival folklore has preserved into the present. For instance, it was customary on the final day of Carnival to burn the simulacra of a giant and a giantess, ritual incarnations of the fat days. La Manekine and her son are the legendary substitutes of these characters.

We should be careful not to assume that the Carnival-like rites mentioned in *La Manekine* are simple literary allusion the author slid into his text. In fact, it is the story of La Manekine herself that constitutes the folklore version (partially Christianized by Philippe de Remy) of an authentic myth of Carnival. With rare precision, the narrative maintains the ritual dates in relation to the myth that it evokes. The parallel testimony provided by folklore enables us to measure the importance of this preserved story.

La Manekine cannot help but call to mind *Peau d'âne* (Donkey Skin): A widowed king wishes to marry his daughter, but to avoid this she covers herself in the hide of an ass and plays the part of a gooseherd until a charming prince finds her and rescues her from her wretched situation. The theme of incest that opens both stories underlines the related fate of the two characters and leads to this question: are La Manekine, missing her hand, and Peau d'âne two fictional avatars reflecting the same mythical character?

In order to answer this question, we should not be confused by the name Peau d'âne. In his sixteenth-century *Contes d'Eutrapel*, Noel du Fail cites the traditional story of *Cuir d'anette* (Duck Skin), the title of which refers to the original name of the story of *Peau d'âne* and makes it impossible for us to doubt her connection to ducks rather than donkeys.

The donkey skin turns out to be not that of a donkey, but rather that of an *anette*, or, in other words, a little *ane* or little *cane* (duck). *Anette*, formed from the Latin *anas*, "duck," was commonly the word used for "duck" in the sixteenth century. *Anette* does not have any lexical relationship to *âne* but does relate to *ane*, *anile*, *enille*, and so forth. We must therefore presume that Peau d'âne was named this because she originally wore the skin of a *cane* (duck), a distinction that makes her akin to the bird-women figures of Celtic mythology. Furthermore, the myth of Carna recalls the existence of bird-women (and ogresses) who have a particular attraction to human flesh, especially that of infants. They no doubt form the Latin analog of the bird-women of Celtic tradition. The word *ane* (or *cane*) can be within the name La Manekine, which might well provide a mythological key to the character. The original form of her name could well have been Anekine, which the thirteenth-century writer reinterpreted as Manekine, no doubt in allusion to her amputated hand (*main* in French). Given that we have no indication that the word *mannequin* existed before the romance *La Manekine*, it could not very well have constituted the etymon of this proper name.

In this regard, it is worthwhile for us to examine certain variations of the story *La Manekine*. The *Revue de l'histoire des religions* has published several Slavic variants of the "daughter with the cut-off hand."[10] These texts offer significant aspects to the study of some thematic analogies present in the myth *Peau d'âne*, especially if we consider the myth not as an original and archetypal text, but rather as a focal point from which the variants of a tradition radiate outward and by which these variants are illuminated.

Certain Russian and Serbian variants on the story of the child of La

Manekine are rightfully described by folklorists as mythical. In these the child is described as being gilded to the elbows, with legs that are silver up to the knees. His forehead bears a red sun and his nape a shining moon. In these same versions, the mother-in-law lies: "Your wife has given birth to a child who is half dog and half bear; she lives in the woods, in the company of beasts," or even "Your mistress and our little girl has given birth to a child like none we have ever seen before: He has the paws of a wolf, the eyes and brow of a bear, and the jaw of a dog." The medieval version confirms these descriptions and adds that the hairy creature to whom La Manekine gives birth has four feet, deep-set eyes, and an enormous head that emerged from its mother's womb and "fled like a *vouivre* (women-serpent), according to the ancient French text. An Occitan version of the story of La Manekine, *Sainte Brigitte,* specifies that "A child was born and the mother responded that she gave birth to something, but didn't really know if it was a dog or a child." This story recalls a monstrous creature that the archaic versions of this same tale probably placed at the heart of the story. Furthermore, this hybrid creature was ritually connected to the date of Carnival. It is customary to find such chimeras in medieval legends. The legend of the Swan Knight clearly tells the tale of human beings transformed into swans that have been passed off as dogs.[11]

This man-dog-bird equivalence can be found in the commemoration of the saints that takes place around Candlemas and Carnival.* There are folk liturgies transpiring near the bonfire of Carnival that have not yet revealed all their mythic secrets. The insight triggered by *La Manekine* demands confirmation by additional analyses that relate primarily to the hagiographic traces of the myth of Carnival.

It is first vital to underscore the importance of the Carnival deity hidden behind the character of La Manekine. She is the key to unlocking our understanding of the hagiographic puzzle constructed around the eight great carnivalesque dates. We will see later that another

---

*[The legend of Saint Brigid, for instance, who is commemorated on February 1, associates her with both a bird and a dog, and birds, it was said, fed Saint Blaise in his hermitage. —*Trans.*]

medieval romance gives the name Garganeüs (reminiscent of Gargantua, the preeminent giant of Carnival) to the monster in the form of a woman-serpent to which La Manekine gives birth. Examined from the mythic angle, we can thus see that La Manekine is none other than the giant—or rather, the giantess—of Carnival, who is burned in the bonfire of Firebrand Sunday.

It is therefore around the bonfire of Carnival that the principal rites and myths of the period are concentrated. In fact, this attention to carnival-style rites demands another reading of the entire legend and folklore tradition of the Middle Ages for the purpose of better understanding the mythological memory that gives it its organization. The convergence of medieval and modern folklore, as well as medieval literary texts and nonliterary mythological and ethnological evidence, makes it possible to restore the "wild" memory of the pre-Christian world and the network of pagan beliefs that are attached to it. A renewed understanding of this medieval literature along with its relationship to folktales is at the heart of this reexamination. While here we cannot undertake an exhaustive exploration of these vast and still largely unexplored domains, we can open some new paths of research.

TWO

November 1, Samhain

A ny journey into the myths and rites of the Middle Ages should begin in the dark season. The great figures that govern all the mythical thought of both medieval Christianity and paganism take shape on the threshold of winter. We will follow such thought in its dual expression: in hagiography and in its literary and folklore form. This study of contrasts is necessary to grasp the specific character of each tradition as well as to underscore the common elements on which these two traditions are based.

Samhain, the Night of Passage

In the ancient Irish calendar, the celebration of November 1 is called Samhain,[1] and the night of November 1 to November 2 is rich in legends that feed on an old reserve of myth that even today is particularly vital in certain regions. This is the time when the beings of the Otherworld have temporary permission to visit the living and is also the moment when the living gain furtive access to the Otherworld.

In Brittany it was fairly common to come across the Cart of the Dead, which carried souls toward their future home. In *La Légende de la mort chez les Bretons armoricains*, Anatole Le Braz has gathered a truly exhaustive survey of the traditions connected to this All Saints' Day funerary cart. It was essential to avoid finding yourself on the same road as the cart unless you also wanted to find yourself in the Otherworld in the company of the terrifying flying host of the Wild Hunt. Breton folklore abounds with traditions that tell of hearing an extraordinary din on the night of November 1. This is the noise of the cart that lurches toward the beyond with its cargo of corpses and ghosts. The devil himself is said to be driving before him this vociferous herd of souls headed to hell once and for all.

In Celtic mythology, the date of Samhain is often invested with the notion of transition or passage, for this is the moment when the beings from the Beyond pay a visit to mortals. It is also the time when the hero Cuchulain is said to have taken part in a fairy hunt during which he slew two birds that, in reality, were two goddesses of the Otherworld transformed into birds.[2] Samhain thus corresponds to a period that favors communication with the *sid,* the Otherworld of Celtic tradition.

The concept of the Otherworld is a central one to Celtic mythology and beliefs. In many regards, it provides the key to an understanding of the rites and myths according to the calendar. Obviously, this Otherworld should not be understood in terms of an exclusively Christian model, although Christian beliefs eventually penetrated it. The Otherworld is the place of choice for ghosts and is primarily the world of fairies, for it is explained by Faery and it explains Faery, which itself is only a lesser form of a divine magic. The Otherworld forms a major theme in literature of Celtic origin and is especially emphasized in medieval Arthurian literature.[3]

In 998, Odilon, the fourth abbot of Cluny, instituted the Commemoration of the Dead, or the Day of the Departed, on November 2. In doing so he was merely adapting to Christianity an old Celtic custom that viewed this time of year as one in which souls engaged in their funerary migration. By placing a holiday dedicated to the dead on this particular day, he diverted toward Christian worship the ancient beliefs of Samhain, which were thus rendered harmless, being now attached to another vision of the Beyond that offered the hope of heaven alongside the threat of hell.

Halloween

Placed at a strategic moment of the calendar, the celebration of November 1 has become conflated with the celebration known in Anglo-Saxon countries as Halloween. This holiday might best be defined as November's Carnival. Indeed, in Anglo-Saxon folklore, Halloween comprises a collection of old beliefs and old rites of communication with the Beyond. Of course, this day gives American children the opportuniy to wear a wide variety of disguises, while at night it often involves the flight of witches in the moonlight.

The night of Halloween, a veritable night of the devil, is marked by a full set of beliefs relating to magic and sorcery. The world of the Faery suddenly topples into the ordinary world—that is, the world of myth abruptly enters the norms of daily life and supernatural forces are unleashed to threaten humans. Several recent films by the director Tommy Lee Wallace have evoked the myths and mysteries of this American holiday tradition marked by sorcery. In *Halloween III,* a man shows up at a California hospital dazed and trembling with fright. A doctor observes that the man panics even more when he catches sight of a television ad for masks. Soon after, a mysterious figure enters the hospital and kills the man before immolating himself. Even more famous, in Steven Spielberg's film *E.T.,* the extraterrestrial appears on earth at the time of Halloween, something like a fairy representative from the Otherworld entering the quotidian world. It is interesting to note that science fiction is often the refuge for a diluted mythology that has as its source the imaginary rhythms of old European myths that are primarily, but not exclusively, Celtic.

First and foremost, Samhain and Halloween pose the existence of an Otherworld (which should not be confused with the world of the Dead or with hell or heaven). The Samhain Otherworld, the source of meaning for all the Samhain rites and myths, is inhabited by fairies and revenants. As with the seven other major dates of the calendar, Samhain and Halloween make it possible to establish a dialogue with the Otherworld by authorizing the emergence of a more or less dangerous magic linked to a reversal of the seasons and a kind of fracture in time.

November 11, Saint Martin's Day

Forty days before Christmas (November 11) is the feast day of Saint Martin, but because of the U.S. and Western European institution of Armistice Day (Veterans Day) on November 11 after World War I, the memory of Saint Martin has been considerably weakened. Yet Saint Martin, known as the apostle of the Gauls, played an essential role (perhaps one more symbolic than real) in the conversion of France to Christianity. His actual historical role is no doubt much less significant than the one attributed to him by his posthumous legend. It is undeniable, however, that this figure gives us a key to understanding the masking of paganism by Christianity starting in the first centuries of evangelization, in the fifth or sixth century.

As we have seen, it was not until this era that the program of Christianization later described by Pope Gregory was put into place. This involved Christianity's annexing of paganism's sacred sites (trees, springs, stones of worship), the establishment of an administrative organization (bishoprics, parishes, and so on), the archiving of pagan memory and the Christian reformulation of ancient mythology into a doctrinal context that conformed to the gospels (which coincided with the appearance of the first hagiographic documents). The importance of a figure like Saint Martin with regard to the Christianization of the countryside has been noted for a long time.[4]

The Saint Martin Stones

There is an abundance of folklore concerning Saint Martin.[5] The places where the saint has left traces of his passage are beyond count. One legend shows the similarity between Saint Martin and Merlin the enchanter, who is well known for having built certain megalithic constructions such as the cromlech of Stonehenge near Avebury, known as the Dance of the Giants. In Vauxrenard (Burgundy), the Stone of Saint Martin is also called the Stone of the Fairies or Stone of the Saracens. The story goes that Saint Martin was competing with the devil in transporting enormous blocks of stone to the top of Mount Gouvry. The devil was on the verge of winning when a miracle occurred: The enormous Stone of Saint Martin was carried to its resting place on a cart hitched to two calves and led by Christ himself.

It happens that there is a large number of Saint Martin stones in France, where the saint is alleged to have left a marked trace of his passage. Near Solre-le-Château (in the administrative region of Nord), one of the Saint Martin stones is said to retain the imprint left by his body after he leaned against it to rest. The Stone of Saint Martin in Perrigny-les-Auxerre is a Celtic remnant that was Christianized with the establishment of Christianity in this region. Saint Martin is said to have left a print of his knees in Dun-les-Places and that of his feet in Vauclais, near Clamechy. The footsteps of the Saint Martin's duck are said to be found carved in a boulder in Lavault-de-Frétoy near Château-Chinon, while a spring supposedly created by the feet of Saint Martin's donkey still flows at a site named Le Pas de l'Âne Caché (Hidden Footsteps of the Donkey) in the canton of Luzy in the Nièvre. Two other Saint Martin stones can be counted in Cuzy, which is also in the Nièvre, and there are many others in a number of regions throughout France. These stones could certainly be seen as the wild imaginings of a folklore suffering from a lack of notoriety—one that looked to give itself value by establishing such physical and "historical" support. Gregory of Tours himself, in the sixth century, consecrated the authority of such evidence in stone; he reports, for example, that in the Basilica of Tours, it was possible to distinguish the stone on which Saint Martin had sat, and that in Nieuls-les-Saintes, at the start of a spring that Martin had caused to gush forth, it was possible to see a stone bearing the print of the hoof of the donkey the bishop was riding.[6] The date of the mentioning of these sites confers on them a great value and compels their examination as tangible signs of an active myth. Even if all the Saint Martin stones were not recognized as such during the sixth century, the fact that two of them were is sufficient to accept the existence of a Martinian folklore during the early Middle Ages and to take into consideration this lore in a mythological study of the saint. While it is quite obvious that these traces should not be studied as historical evidence, they must be noted as the memory's traces of a myth that are related.

Throughout France and the rest of Europe, other saints and illustrious figures are supposed to have left similar imprints on stones, suggesting the survival of old mythic beliefs that, over the years, human imagination has applied to saints or heroes. In the twelfth century, the writer Béroul mentions the Stone of Saut Tristan in Cornwall, where, it was said, Tristan left his footprints. As with this place in Cornwall, beneath a site glides the image of a myth maintained by the shadow of a rite. For ages people have come to such stones to pray for the birth of a child or for healing, as if these natural monuments were the true containers of the power of life thanks to the "holy" memory that has given them life.

In truth, the Saint Martin stones together constitute the popular version of a mythology the written traces of which are often slender and a matter for careful interpretation, but which nevertheless exists as a major European mythology. Even if it did not craft a culture as brilliant as the Hellenic or Roman world, the Celtic world has contributed to the development of Western culture for several millennia. It is impossible for a contribution of this magnitude to utterly disappear at the time of the Roman invasion or as a result of the conversion of peoples to Christianity. To the contrary, it melted into the Mediterranean and Christian cultures, influencing them in ways that, while intangible, have been undoubtedly enriching.

The Martin Bear

The Martin Bear is a well-known figure in folk tradition. For our purposes, we will focus on this figure to explain the relation it established between the figure of the bear and that of Saint Martin. Only medieval mythology enables us to precisely clarify this mythical aspect of the saint.

First, it is striking to note that on November 9, two days prior to Saint Martin's Day on November 11, is the feast day of Saint Ursinus, the first bishop of Bourges, whose name obviously derives from the Latin *ursus,* meaning "bear." The Benedictines vainly strove to assert that his was a widespread Roman name, but they could not erase the fact that this name is all the more unusual for being borne by a number of saints who did not live in ancient Rome. In addition to this Ursinus of Bourge, there are others that are celebrated on October 2, August 14, June 19, and July 24; an Ursicinus celebrated on December 1; an Urciscenus whose day is June 21; an Ursmer celebrated on April 19; and an Ursula with a feast day of October 21. Indeed, there are so many bears celebrated at different times of the year that it seems as though we are on the trail of a bear calendar!

Symbolically, the bear can be suggestive of a human, and this human appearance has conferred upon it a truly mythical aura.[7] For the Indians of North America, the bear—like us, a plantigrade—was regarded as a brother to the human. Additonally, easily proved in its skinning, the bear's anatomy appeared similar to that of a human. During the Middle Ages, its kinship with man was emphasized in the knowledge that it was the only animal to make love lying down, like humans. The figure of the bear merges with that of the Wild Man, whose archetypal portrait has been drawn by Richard Bernheimer: "It is a hairy man curiously compounded of human and animal traits, without, however, sinking to the level of an ape. It exhibits upon its naked anatomy a growth of fur, which leaves bare only its face, feet, and hands, at times its knees and elbows, or the breasts of the female of the species. Frequently, the creature is shown wielding a heavy club or mace, or the trunk of a tree."[8] This kind of portrait can be found repeatedly in the products of the medieval imaginal realm; for example, it corresponds to several legendary figures encountered in the twelfth-century romances of Chrétien de Troyes.

In fact, the Wild Man become quite a vital myth in the medieval world, also making its appearance in certain court ballets taking place during Carnival festivities. The famous *Bal des Ardents,* peformed at the court of Charles VI in 1392, ended in tragedy: The Wild Men costumes of several courtiers, made of feather, fur, and pitch, managed to catch fire, and all died horribly in the burning.[9]

A song by the troubadour Bernard Sicart de Marvejols contributes some very enlightening mythical evidence about this Wild Man who laughs when it rains and weeps when it is sunny. Contrary to other men, this creature acts and reacts as his madness wills. Yet this disconcerting feature is often the sign of the highest intelligence. In *Yvain ou le Chevalier au Lion* by Chretien de Troyes, Yvain meets a strange creature in the forest of Broceliande:

> I saw that his head was bigger than that of a horse or of any other beast; that his hair was in tufts, leaving his forehead bare for a width of more than two spans; that his ears were big and mossy, just like those of an elephant; his eyebrows were heavy and his face was flat; his eyes were those of an owl, and his nose was like a cat's; his jowls were split like a wolf, and his teeth were sharp and yellow like a wild boar's; his beard was black and his whiskers twisted; his chin merged into his chest and his backbone was long, but twisted and hunched. There he stood, leaning upon his club, accoutred in a strange garb consisting not of cotton or wool, but rather of the hides recently flayed from two bulls or two beeves.[10]

In fact, this rustic of such bestial appearance or this composite animal of human appearance was none other than a seer who held knowledge of the secret science of places and animals. He revealed to Yvain the hidden path that led to the marvelous fountain of Barenton. He also demonstrated his exceptional power over angry bulls, for he managed to gain mastery over these enraged animals simply by grabbing them by their horns. This ability makes him akin to the major Indo-European deity who is the guardian of the divine pasturage and the god of livestock, serpents, and the dead.

The Wild Man is the folkloric form of an ancient Celtic deity who survived into the Middle Ages through incorporation into saints like Blaise and Martin and the figure of the wizard Merlin.[11] If we look closely at the legendary life of Saint Martin, we might determine that he is an old Celtic figure with a name close to Merlin's who has been covered with a Christian cloak. The phonetic proximity of the two names alone provides justification for a comparison that can be confirmed by studying certain motifs borrowed from medieval hagiographic documents.

The *Life of Saint Martin,* written by Sulpicius Severus, alludes to the saint's odd talents, which smack more of the seer, the magician, or the wizard than a being inhabited solely by divine grace. For example, the account tells that one day, while on the road, Saint Martin encountered the funeral procession of a pagan. He halted at a certain distance to watch the mourners who followed the shroud-covered body and was immediately reminded of a familiar Gallic pagan ceremony: "He believed that some profane rites of sacrifice were being performed. This thought occurred to him, because it was the custom of the Gallic rustics, in their wretched folly, to carry about through the fields the images of demons veiled with a white covering."[12]

When Martin next made the sign of the cross, everyone in the procession abruptly froze in place as if each had been petrified. They tried to resume their progress, but could only spin around until they dropped onto the ground the corpse they were carrying. Martin then realized he had made a mistake and allowed the cortege to continue its march.

This hagiographic text is based on a curious juxtaposition of pagan beliefs and Christianity and sometimes even the commingling of the two. Martin, the saint invested with divine power, plays the sorcerer by paralyzing a troop of respectable mourners he mistakes for miscreants. His magical power to petrify is comparable to that employed by the ancient Gorgons. Despite his suspicions of the mourners, it is finally he who displays the most alarming powers, while they turn out to be entirely innocent. In Martin we can see peeking through the figure of the saint the persona of a magician that has emerged directly from Celtic paganism.

Saint Martin and Saint Hilairius

If we believe his legend, Saint Martin was far from a bear or the archetypal Wild Man. Yet his hagiographers portray him as somewhat wild, with his ugly tonsure, his mean clothing, and his predilection for rustic places—all signs of a certain refusal of the civilized world and a natural affinity to a more wild lifestyle. A "bear" could definitely hide itself quite easily within this very unconventional bishop. As if to place stronger emphasis on the strangeness of his powers, *The Golden Legend* stresses Martin's aptitude for miracles: he exorcised a cow that was enraged and tormented by a demon, he recognizes all the demons and calls them by name, and he naturally knows how to command animals. These are all features that betray his kinship to the likes of Merlin the Enchanter in the Arthurian legend or the villein of Broceliande in Chrétien de Troyes's work.

After being converted to Christianity, Martin was ordained as a priest by Saint Hilairius and founded numerous religious establishments, including the Ligugé Abbey near Poitiers. Could the name of this site tell of its devotion to the Celtic god Lug, and could Martin thus essentially be the alibi for the Christianization of a pagan site? In any event, we must note Martin's association with a saint whose name in Latin means "laugher" (*hilaris*). What is certainly hiding beneath this apparently anodyne connection and the saint himself is the seer's eternal aptitude for prophetic laughter, the perfect literary image of which we find in Merlin.[13] In fact, in the Arthurian romances, the laughter of Merlin always corresponds to the ritual phase of his prophecies. This is a mystical laughter, an inspired laughter that is also the laughter of Carnival. From Hilairius to Martin, proper names often yield barely perceptible but nonetheless recognizable traces of a mythical presence, if we pay heed to the convergence of date and name.

Through this mythical connection to date, Merlin appears as the tutelary figure standing (and not without reason) on the threshold of the time of Carnival. Tradition never misses any opportunity to confirm that the festival begins on the eleventh day of the eleventh month—or on Saint Martin's Day.

Saint Martin's Goose

The feast of Saint Martin was among the major celebrations of the Middle Ages and was equal in importance to the feast of Saint John. Bonfires comparable to the fires of Saint John were lit on the eve of November 11 in Flanders, Brabant, the Rhineland, and Luxembourg. Saint Martin's Day was also an occasion to eat and drink generously. In part because of this unrestrained celebration, the Council of Auxerre in 578 sought to put an end to the festivities in honor of this saint. Their efforts were apparently unsuccessful, however, for in the sixteenth century Ronsard continued to celebrate the "Martins" in the purest Bacchic tradition. If we are to believe Rabelais, the verb *martiner* (formed from the name Martin) meant "to drink a lot": *Parquoy ung chascun de l'armée se mist a martiner, chopiner et tringuer des mesmes*[14] (As a consequence, each man in the army began to tipple, to ply the pot and swill it down).

Is it possible that Martin was invested with some sort of Gargantuan and Pantagruelian dimension to authorize such libations in his honor? Included among the ritual dishes of Saint Martin are a fatted goose (or chicken) and crescent-shaped cakes called Saint Martin's horns, which also clearly bring to mind the affection of the Wild Man for horned animals or for the crescent moon. As for the Wild Man's association to the bull and birds, confirmation of the incorporation of this affinity into Christianity is provided by the Gallic statue of the *tarvos trigaranos* (bull with three cranes) that was discovered buried on the site of Notre Dame in Paris. The use of these animals summons up a religious extension of the theme that can find its source only in the context of Celtic mythology.

Saint Martin holds the role of an eminent French saint. The greatest number of French churches (close to four thousand) are dedicated to him and the places that begin with or include Saint Martin in their name are beyond count. This kind of celebrity cannot be the work of chance. If we are to believe the official legend of Martin, this son of a retired Legionnaire, born in Sabaria in Hungary, offered half of his cloak on one particularly harsh winter day to a vagabond who was wandering the streets of Amiens. On returning to the barracks with only half his cloak, he had to endure the gibes of his fellows, but his gift definitively connected his name to a legendary charity. This hagiographic motif could easily be understood within the context of folklore traditions and folktales.

One surprising element of Martin's presentation is the presence of a donkey at his side. We would rather expect to seem him riding a horse, which is definitely more effective in battle. Yet folklore does not burden itself with logic but instead preserves the features of a secular tradition. The memory of Saint Martin is combined with that of the donkey. Yet the form of the word *donkey* (*âne*) seems to have been preserved almost independent of its meaning, for the *ane* (duck) of Saint Martin in not quite an *âne* (donkey). As we have seen earlier and as we will confirm in our study of other legendary and mythical figures, the word *ane* can have two meanings in ancient French. This term designates not only the equine creature (from the Latin word *asinus*) that is well known for its whims and stubbornness, but also a duck or goose via a linguistic line of descent from the Latin word *anas*. Hence, the ritual goose of Saint Martin is explained in *ane*—donkey or duck.

It is helpful to add a folklore fact to this linguistical observation: In Alsace, in the Munster Valley, there is a kind of female Father Christmas, a Christmas Lady who distributes sweets to children in the company of an *âne à bec* (donkey with a beak). This beaked donkey is nothing other than a duck, a fairy tale creature from the Otherworld, a bird-woman like the others we find in the mythic tales of Celtic origin and in the folktales they have spawned. According to a Latin biography of Merlin (*Vita Merlini*) dating from the twelfth century, the fairy Morgan knew the art of flying through the air. She can be easily connected to the long lineage of bird-women, sovereign goddesses who, like wizards, are the keepers of magic powers.

On November 11, Saint Martin, riding his donkey, distributes gifts to children in certain regions of Germany, Austria, and Belgium. In Germany, Holland, and Lorraine it is Saint Nicholas, also on a donkey, who brings joy to the hearts of youngsters. In Wales there is a mythical horse called Aderyn bee y llwyd (bird with the gray beak) that makes the rounds of all the houses on Christmas and New Year's Day—quite reminiscent of the beaked donkey from the Alsatian valleys. All of these figures were eventually replaced by Father Christmas, himself the heir of the Anglo-Saxon Santa Claus, linked by name to Nicholas, who himself leads a donkey bearing gifts when legend does not have him pulled by swans or reindeer. And all of these figures are linked to an ancient bird-woman figure bequeathed by the Celtic great goddess, a provider of sovereignty and wealth who symbolically arrives to offer her presents at the time of the gift-giving and festive season—that is, at the time when time is renewed, the dawn of the new year. In the game of snakes and ladders,* the sacred bird guides the player through eighty-one squares toward the end of an initiatory journey, just like the goose of Saint Martin, who knows the secrets of the Otherworld.

The official hagiographic texts on Saint Martin in their way (and without explicitly admitting it) confirm this obscure connection of the saint to the Otherworld as well as to the fairylike world of the bird-women or the great goddess of the Celts. Sulpicius Severus relates how Saint Martin took refuge for a time on Gallinaria (meaning "henhouse" in Latin) Island, which is located in the Tyrrhenian Sea. From this it would seem that Martin's contact with geese and ducks (or *anes*) was quite commonly known and recalled but carefully hidden. In reality, the theme of Martin's consort, the bird-goddess of the Otherworld, is central to our understanding of the mythical pre-Christian figure who was overlaid with the figure of the saint.

A rereading of the Amiens episode of the cloak Martin cut in half can confirm the presence of coded mythological motifs. Folk stories, in fact, offer many instances comparable to this charity of Saint Martin, the motif of the young man who has nothing but gladly and generously does a favor for someone who begs his aid. Most often in the hagiography the person in need of assistance is Christ himself or the Virgin in disguise, while in folktales he or she is most often a fairy in disguise. To reward the benefactor, the fairy (or Christ or the Virgin) gives to the one who has helped a magic object—most often a talisman (a chain or wand, for instance) or an animal (a golden goose). For example, three collected versions of story type 571 are entitled *The Golden Goose:* The

---

*[The French name for this game, now popularly known as chutes and ladders, is *jeu de l'oie*, literally translated as "goose game."—*Trans.*]

charitable young man (Saint Martin, for instance) can own a goose (*ane*) that will earn him eternal riches (or eternal life, in the case of Saint Martin). The theme of the shared cloak thus belongs to a mythical series partially concealed by the hagiographic story but perfectly legible in the context of Celtic myth, folklore, and hagiography, forming a veritable hierophany.

Saint Hubertus and the Stag

In the marvelous world of medieval hagiographic legends, another animal symbolizes the temporary liaison Samhain allows between the human world and the enchanted world of the fairies: the stag, which is also associated with Saint Hubertus, whose feast day is celebrated on November 3.

The life of Saint Hubertus, son of Bertand, duke of Aquitaine, is well known to hunters, who have chosen him as their patron saint.[15] Hubertus had such a passion for hunting that even on Good Friday he devoted himself to his favorite pastime in the Ardennes forests. As legend tells, on this particular day, as if to signify to Hubertus the sacrilege he is committing, a large stag he is pursuing turns around and faces him. Between its antlers the stag bears the image of Christ on the cross with this inscription: "How long will you allow this vain passion to lead you to neglect the salvation of your soul?" At the same moment, a voice cries out: "Contemplate your salvation. Abandon this worldly life." Overwhelmed, the young prince throws away his hunting weapon and, grasping the enormity of his sin, seeks to repent through a life of mortification at the monastery of Stavelot in Belgium. Hubertus subsequently became the bishop of Tongres and Masstricht, was elevated to sainthood, and became an eminent healer of rabies in men and animals.

The legend of Saint Hubertus appears as the Christian rewriting of a tale that can be corroborated countless times in the medieval literature of Celtic origin. These tales concern the encounter of a human and an animal (a white doe or stag) that is the animal guise of a creature from the Otherworld—that is, a fairy. Here we see again the animal consort that we find in the stories of Saint Martin. The tale of Guigemar, told by Marie de France in the twelfth century,[16] offers a purely profane version of this mythical adventure: The young knight Guigemar goes to the forest one day to indulge in his favorite sport of hunting. All at once he spies in some thick bushes a white doe "with stag's antlers on her head." He shoots an arrow that strikes the animal, but this same arrow turns back toward the hunter and sorely wounds him. The doe then speaks, confessing her sorrow while warning Guigemar of the fate that awaits him.

In the Chrtistianized legend of Saint Hubertus,[17] the stag-fairy has become an avatar of Christ. Retaining its gift of speech, it can influence the destiny of the person who encounters it by converting the sinner to the Faith or by revealing to the young, innocent man the truths of love. In both cases, the stag plays the role of an animal psychopomp, leading an all-too-human figure toward his ultimate truth. He especially has served as a mediator between the human world and the Otherworld at a critical time of transition and passage: Samhain.

The legend of Finn, the Irish hero who bears the name Stag, is directly associated with the rites of the magic hunt. One day in the forest he comes across a doe that has taken shelter near him. Finn brings her to his fortress and the doe is transformed into a young girl, who confesses to him that she was the victim of a curse placed on her by a black druid. Finn marries her, but the black druid manages to steal the girl from the hero's guard and transforms her back into a doe. Later, while hunting, Finn meets a young boy who claims he has been reared by a doe. Finn recognizes his own son and gives him the name Ossian (fawn). Subsequently, Finn's grandson is called Oscar (he who loves the stags). In Finn's legend, as in the legend of Saint Hubertus, the doe-fairy belongs to the Otherworld and serves to pass on the echo of an ancient deity promised an ephemeral existence among mortals. Undoubtedly her passage among humans corresponds to the ritual dates on which the stag and Saint Hubertus are celebrated.

We can note that stag costumes are a common part of the regalia of Carnival—and from earliest times they prompted the disapproval of the clergy. Cesaire of Arles condemned it, as did Bishop Faustin, who bellowed: "What man of healthy mind would believe men of healthy minds could disguise themselves as stags and transform into wild beasts? Some dress in skins and others wear animal heads; and they dance and jump as if they were transformed into wild beasts and were no longer men." A sixteenth-century miniature depicts this stag disguise: The wearer is facing a musician holding a fife and drum. We must accept the permanent place of these Carnival costumes throughout the course of the centuries despite all the efforts deployed by the Church to eliminate them.

The words *horn* and *stag* are related to the Celtic god Cernunnos. On the Gundestrup Cauldron, a veritable condensed iconographic index of Celtic mythology, we find this horned god surrounded by various animals and numerous fertility and wealth symbols. Yet this figure may well harken to even older, perhaps shamanic beliefs that preceded the Celtic world. The first people in the West were in fact consumers and hunters of deer, as is testified to by cave paintings.

The god with the stag's head reappears in Carnac, disguised as Saint Cornély, who is always depicted with a horned bull.* During the pardon of Saint Cornély in the month of September, a procession takes place during which horned animals are brought before the priest so they can receive his blessing. Saint Cornély is the protector of horned animals in all of southern Brittany.

Another saint with a relationship to the stag is Edern, whose name brings to mind that of the knight Yder in the Arthurian cycle. The legend recounts how Edern quarrels with his sister Genoveva about the territory they are to settle when they arrive in Great Britain. Edern and his sister decide to mark the boundaries of their respective lands by riding a stag. The animal thereby becomes the guarantor of a rite of foundation and plays his boundary-establishing role admirably. At the conjunction of the two worlds (the real world and the Otherworld) and the two times (human time and Faery time), the stag remains the initiatory animal par excellence, revealing the path and truth of the Otherworld.

---

*[The name Saint Cornély has within it the French word for horn: *corne*. —*Trans.*]

The major dates of the mythical calendar allow for intense exchanges with the Otherworld, as Samhain admirably demonstrates. All the myths connected to the feasts whose cycles are opened by Samhain recount to one degree or another the communication between the Otherworld and the human world. Thus, the major dates of the mythological calendar—most particularly Samhain—led to the emergence of the Faery into the world of daily life. If even today there is a trivial association of All Saints' Day with cemeteries and commemorating the dead, it is because in our obsure mythical memory bank the date of November 1 remains connected to the passage of souls and ghosts between the two worlds. This is the time when the cart of the dead can be seen in Brittany, and it reappears during the second major Carnival: Christmas. Christmas Eve commemorates the apparition of a revenant called Father Christmas, who travels through the air on a sleigh pulled by reindeer. Saint Martin thus announces the second great stage in the mythological cycle.

THREE

Christmas and the Twelve Days

F orty days after Samhain (All Saints' Day), the holiday of Christmas in conjunction with Saint Sylvester's Day (December 31) is marked by a set of pagan customs that Christianity has not entirely succeeded in smothering. In truth, Christmas unlocks the door to a key period of the calendar and some important rites in the Middle Ages: The period known as the Twelve Days, extending from December 25 to January 6 (Epiphany), is characterized by a collection of rites and myths of unknown origin that have survived into the present day. Ignorance of medieval traditions partially explains the inconsistency of historians' explanations regarding these rites and legends.

For Christians, Christmas celebrates the birth of Jesus. Yet this anniversary was placed at different times of the year before being fixed at December 25. In different eras, in accordance with various Christian religions, Christmas was variously attached to January 6, March 25, April 10, and May 29. The commemoration of Christ's birth on December 25 resulted from seasonal and mythological associations to pagan beliefs that are older than Christianity.

The Meal of the Fairies and the Eve Celebrations

The celebrations of Christmas Eve and Saint Sylvester are, even today, the most apparent pagan rites of the end of the year. They valorize the forces of the night as well as the powers of the mysterious and the marvelous. Associated with these is the well-known motif of the fairy meal found in certain medieval texts and folktales.

We saw earlier that Burchard of Worms's eleventh-century *Penitential* mentioned the feast of New Year's Day as a superstitious custom. This is not the earliest mention of such a feast; a ninth-century penitential speaks of a celebration organized in honor of the Parcae (the Fates) at this same time of the year.[1] Another, later text mentions the distinctive appearance of this ritual meal: "You have done in your home what certain women have the custom of doing at certain periods of the year: You set a table in your home and placed upon it the food and drink you have prepared, three plates, and three knives to offer refreshment, if they came, to those three sisters who are ceaselessly perpetuated by an ancient foolishness that calls them the Parcae."

The meal of the Parcae presumes, in fact, the ritual arrival of the fairies "at certain times of the year." As the texts say, they come so that they may find hospitality that will subsequently encourage them to hand out their gifts. These fairies visit the houses, examine the foodstuffs that are set out, and satiate their hunger. If the meals earn their approval, they bestow favors upon their hosts. This is confirmed by a testimony from the thirteenth-century folklorist Gervase of Tilbury:

> The same can be said about the spirit which, in the guise of a woman, visits homes and pantries during the night in the company of other women who is named Satia, satiety, and also Dame Habonde because of the abundance she is said to confer upon the homes she visits. This is the same kind of spirits that the old wives call dames, and about whom they maintain this error to which credence is given even in illusory dreams: These old wives say that the dames use up the food and drink they find in homes without consuming it utterly or even reducing its quantity, especially if the dishes holding these foods are left uncovered and if those vessels holding drinks are not corked when left out for the night. But if they are found covered, sealed, or corked, the dames will abandon these houses to unhappiness and misfortune without granting them satiety or abundance.[2]

In *Roman de la Rose,* Jean de Meun classifies as superstition these nocturnal wanderings in the company of Dame Habonde:

> Many people in their folly think themselves to be witches wandering the night with Dame Habonde; they tell how one in three children share her ability to go out three times during the week; they force themselves in every house, fearing neither keys nor bars, entering by the chinks, cat holes, and cracks. Their souls, leaving their bodies, go with the Good Ladies through houses and yards, and they offer to prove it by saying that the oddities they witnessed never come to them in their beds so it must be that their souls were thus acting and running in the world.[3]

These nocturnal voyages represent the vast quantity of phantasmagoria concerning witches and wizards that invaded the imagination of the late Middle Ages. After the thirteenth century, the Sabbat accumulated in its imaginary contents a sum of decomposing pagan beliefs and myths that contributed mythical features closely related to the Celtic world. Ever on the lookout for magical beliefs that could serve its needs, the Church tried to divert the suggestive powers contained in pagan myths. It founded a cult to Mary on a site haunted by fairies. The pilgrimage to Notre-Dame-d'Abondance, near Evian, thus places under the authority of the Virgin the ancient powers of Dame Habonde, as we can see through the works of medieval authors, and transferred the powers of the fairy to the Virgin Mary.

Despite the ambivalence (beneficial and malicious) of the fairy figure that should serve as its guarantor, the New Year's Day meal possesses a well-defined votive character. It aims to appropriate the beneficial forces that govern the cycles of time and permit the advent of fertility and prosperity. Receiving a visit from the fairies on this day was a good omen for the coming year. Such beliefs persisted well beyond the sixteenth century.

In fact, the continuity between medieval traditions concerning this visit and modern folklore has been conclusively esstablished. A. Maury mentions one such Pyrenees custom:

The fairies (*hadas*) enter the homes of those who worship them, carrying good fortune in their right hand and misfortune in their left. One must take pains to prepare the meal that should be offered to them in a clean and isolated room. The doors and windows are opened and a white tablecloth is placed on the table along with a loaf of bread, a knife, a vessel full of water and wine, and a cup. A candle or taper should sit in the center of the table. It is generally believed that those who offer them the best dishes can hope to see their herds increased, their harvests abundant, and the fulfillment of the dearest wishes related to the nuptial bond; whereas those who only reluctantly perform their duties toward the fairies and who neglect to make preparations worthy of them, should expect great misfortune. At daybreak on January 1, the father, the elder, the master of each house takes back the bread that was offered to the fairies and, after dipping it into the wine and water, distributes it to his entire family and even the servants. Thus, wishes for a happy new year are made and one breakfasts on this bread.[4]

Although Christianity did not maintain the custom of this meal with the fairies on New Year's Day, we might wonder if the ritual of the Eucharist somehow substituted for this, remodeling its imaginary arrangement. A midnight Mass is celebrated on Christmas, one of the two occasions in the year when Mass (which theoretically should always be performed in broad daylight) can be celebrated in the middle of the night. Perhaps this Midnight Mass supplanted the pagan rite of a communion meal with beings from the Otherworld. The common presence of bread and wine both in the fairies' meal and in the rite of Christian Communion serves to underscore a reference to the same sacred rite, one being placed under divine authority and the other under that of the fairies. Here again, Christianity borrowed pagan tradition and conferred upon it a new spiritual dimension.

We should also note another characteristic of the fairy meal in medieval tradition: According to several literary texts, the meal with fairies is also held at the birth of certain predestined children. This is why fairies show up on the night of the birth of heroes such as Ogier the Dane and William Short Nose, in order to endow these children with great virtues. Thus it it seems entirely natural to fix the Nativity of Christ on this night of the Mothers (or night of the fairies) on which the birth of profane heroes was already celebrated. The setting of Christmas on December 25 seems a clear association with the pagan custom of attaching the fairy repast to the birth of an exceptional individual. Indeed, many rites of Christmas find mythical counterparts in the folk memory that associated this predestined date with the world of Faery.

December 31, Saint Sylvester's Day

Christmas Eve and New Year's Eve appear as the "twins" of the same solstice-based pagan celebration. Both are nights of great danger during the course of which the tutelary presences—revenants—of the Other-world can manifest. The name Sylvester comes from the Latin *sylva,* "forest," and Sylvester is comparable to the figure of the Wild Man, a key figure of pre-Christian mythology and an archetype of the revenant in medieval tradition. Obviously, nothing in the life of this poor pope from the fourth century accounts for his savage name.* Yet it was customary in the countryside to invoke his aid when threatened by an animal. This power Sylvester held over the animal world makes it easy for us to glimpse the pagan background of his worship, especially as connected to his feast day.

Contemporary Romans celebrate Saint Sylvester's Day and New Year's Day by throwing out the window their chipped and broken dishes. They also set off firecrackers or shoot guns, much as other Europeans do on this day. We can note the same customs in Denmark, but their stated purpose is to drive away the elves and all the evil spirits that are particularly active on this night and to keep them from causing harm during the year to come.

---

*[In medieval times, the forest was viewed as savage, rather than benign. The hedge was the boundary separating the tamed lands from the wild forestlands. —*Trans.*]

Another saint whose feast day is celebrated at year's end (December 25) is Saint Anastasia, and her story might explain in part the din (breaking china, firecrackers) associated with the celebration of Saint Sylvester's Day: *The Golden Legend* somewhat humorously recounts her imaginary rape by a Roman prefect: "Believing he was assaulting the Virgin, he embraced the casseroles, the stew pots, the cauldrons, and the cooking utensils." All these are utensils are used during the *charivaris*** and other customs marking the arrival of the New Year. "When he came back to his senses," the text continues, "he emerged all black with dirt and his clothing in shreds. His servants who were waiting for him at the door, seeing him in such a state and believing him changed into a demon, greeted him with a storm of blows, then fled leaving him alone."

This hagiographic text transposes into the context of the Twelve Days those charivari rites practiced precisely at the end of the year. As we will see later, the fourteenth-century *Roman de Fauvel* provides the profane illustration of these charivari customs. The din of Saint Sylvester's Day has no reason for its existence other than maintaining these noisy practices at the time of year when they are expected to assume their imaginary power.

The Wild Hunt

No medieval text is more explicit on the subject of the din associated with revenants than the one recounting the advent of the Mesnie Hellequin during New Year's Eve. An extract for the year 1092 from the Norman chronicle *The Ecclesiastical History of Orderic Vital* makes it possible to rediscover the medieval mythological figure of Hellequin through the thundering Wild Hunt he was said to control. Hellequin is the name given to the "household" of the king and lord of the Otherworld accompanied by his band of warriors, who were greedy for corpses. Appearing in this terrifying parade, accompanied by a deafening commotion, is a

---

*[Charivari is the noisy "serenade" (often involving banging on pots and pans) to a just-wedded couple. —*Trans.*]

figure bearing a strange resemblance to numerous revenants and creatures of the Otherworld evoked by the great literary texts of the Middle
Ages. In reality, this text depicts the central figure of all the medieval
mythology.

According to the medieval historian Orderic Vital, during the night
of December 31 to January 1, 1092 (Saint Sylvester's Night), the priest
of Bonneval (in the Orne region) was returning home after visiting the
sick when he suddenly heard a terrifying fracas and saw a flying army
coming toward him. He tried to conceal himself near four medlar trees
when a man of imposing size armed with a club forced the priest to
stand at his side. An entire wild army filed past the eyes of the terrified
priest. First came the infantrymen, carrying the fruits of their pillage.
Then followed the grave diggers, carrying fifty coffins; the giant with
the club accompanied them. Women on horseback followed, blaspheming and confessing their crimes; then came clerics, abbots, and bishops
pleading with the priest to pray for them. And then again still more
victims. The priest quickly grasped that this was the Mesnie Hellequin
in which he had never wanted to believe, despite the testimonies he had
heard concerning it. The priest sought to step in to the procession and
stop one of the horses, but he burned his hand when he touched the harness. He subsequently fell ill, and the author of this chronicle claims to
have seen his atrocious burns.[5]

The tradition recorded by Orderic Vital contains a composite of
both pagan and Christian elements. A Christian patina covers the most
authentically pagan motifs, and this Christianization of the myth is obvious. The appearance of the tormented sinners brings to mind a kind of
ambulant Purgatory in which the guilty souls are forced to suffer punishment for their earthly crimes.

Yet this Christian dimension is not strong enough to erase the pagan
substratum. The presence of dark-skinned "Ethiopians" exposes the
actual appearance of fairylike, demonic creatures of a mythical black-
ness. They are in fact the incarnation of revenants, a medieval literary or
hagiographic representation of beings of the Otherworld.

The infernal commotion accompanying the cavalcade of revenants is alone sufficient indication of its demonic and insane nature. Finally, the presence of the giant with the club exposes a deity of the Otherworld that easily recalls the famous god with the mallet in Celtic tradition. In Irish mythology, this figure with the club is the Dagda (the good god); one end of his weapon kills while the other resurrects. In all these cases we clearly find ourselves in the presence of a divine figure, that of the Great Demiurge, who Julius Caesar indicated was the principal god of the Gauls.

There can be no doubt as to the unbroken thread of the motif of the Wild Hunt in the beliefs and folklore that have come down to the modern era from the early Middle Ages. Orderic Vital's twelfth-century text is comparable to relatively modern folk traditions[6] as well as a passage from the *Life of Saint Samson,* from the seventh century, that corroborates the existence of this most likely even older belief.

Alain Fournier, the author of *Le Grand Meaulnes,** was a native of Berry and knew the tradition of the Chasse Gayère (Gayère Hunt), another name for the Chasse Gallery, Chasse Arthur, or Mesnie Hellequin. One evening, while he was taking part in a vigil in the cottage of some friends, a terrifying noise startled the guests and held them petrified for a long moment. Only the young son of the master of the house got up. After opening the window, hollered out: "Gayère! Leave on your hunt and go to the devil!" The commotion only grew stronger and bones began falling through the chimney into the fireplace and, on contact with the flames, gave off a pestilential odor that filled the entire cottage.

The legends concerning the Black Hunter, whose wild hunts ceaselessly haunt the forests of all Europe, share these same beliefs. According to certain chroniclers, King Charles VI met him in the forest of Le Mans. This supposedly was the cause of his madness, if we can believe these testimonies.

We might doubt the ancient nature of these beliefs if it was not for

*[An English translation exists (London: Viking Penguin, 2000) under the same title. —*Trans.*]

the existence of an entirely identical story in the *Life of Saint Samson* that adapts the same mythical elements.[7] According to the legend, the saint set off on a journey and was crossing through a forest in the company of a young deacon. Suddenly, the two travelers heard a piercing scream that tore through the forest air. In a panic, the young deacon fled, while Samson remained and made the sign of the cross. He then spied a shaggy, red-haired witch who was holding a hunting spear with three tines and gave the impression that she was flying through the forest. Samson pursued the old witch, which the Latin text describes as a *theomacha* (giantess), and managed to destroy her, but not without having squeezed from her several secrets about her magical origin.

This figure in the air taking part in an eternal hunt in the forest is none other than the deity of the Otherworld who rules the Wild Hunt. Sometimes a woman and sometimes a man, her or his most characteristic feature is a gigantic aspect. The giant, the preeminent mythical figure, thus finds itself at the heart of the myth of the Wild Twelve Days. By virtue of his or her highly ambiguous value, this figure is both a sovereign of the Beyond (master of the passage to death) and a dispenser of life and fertility.

Father Christmas

In the domain of folklore, the flying Wild Hunt announces in reverse the flight of Santa Claus's sleigh pulled by reindeer. As for Santa Claus himself, he is simply the good-natured avatar of a mythical figure, a true distributor of abundance during the middle of winter and supreme master of temporal transitions. Santa Claus is nothing other than the beneficent figure of the Wild Man, the fairy figure from the Otherworld who periodically visits men to give them gifts.

Christmas is obviously a favorable time for the appearance of supernatural beings such as Santa Claus and Father Christmas. In his book *Le Problème des Centaures,* Georges Dumézil gives a fine analysis of "horse play," the promenade of a man-horse "through a village, going from farm to farm, in search of gifts such as simple wheat, oats, eggs, cheese, lard, sausages, smoked meats, eau-de-vie . . ." The custom of this promenade is practiced at certain dates that are well known for their carnival-style rites:

> In Prussia, for example, in Rombitten, the man with the horse head promenades two or four times several days before Christmas, while in Natangen the horse (accompanied by a goat) promenades on Saint Sylvester's Day, and in Tempelbuch the play is reserved for the Carnival that gives it its name. In Hanover the celebration takes place on Christmas, as it does in Bavaria, and the disguise in certain towns is truly a Fastnachtschimmel, a "Carnival horse." In other parts of Germany there are even indications of the horse appearing during Advent, and in Silesia it appears as early as November 10. In Lusace the promenade of the horse takes place on Christmas, then again and mainly at the time of Carnival, or even "from Christmas to Carnival."[8]

The variation in these dates only underscores the permanent nature of this recurring myth. In emphasizing the ritual and mythological equivalence of the eight Carnival-like periods of the year, we can conclude that the game of the horse is a kind of carnival rite and that the horse itself belongs to the rites and myths of this transitional period. As for the name Hellequin itself, no satisfying etymology has so far been proposed. Yet if we consider all the corroborated versions of this name, we find forms such as Hennequin and even Annequin. It so happens that *ene* or *ane* refers to "bird" in old French (we can recall the aerial nature of this hunt), whereas the word *quin* is strongly reminiscent of the word for dog (*kyn-* is the Greek stem meaning "dog"). Perhaps, then, we can read the name Hennequin as "bird-dog." This interpretation offers the advantage of providing a mythical basis to the legendary cynocephalic beings, those figures with the heads of dogs, which may well be the origin of such figures as the dog-headed giant of Saint Christopher, who is also a guide of souls. A legend of the Wild Hunt specific to Armoricain Brittany offers the significant association of the bird and the dog in a folk version of this same myth. It recounts that one evening, a spinner spied a woman flying through the air like a bird, pursued by a white dog and a black dog. Here we see again that the bird and the dog are the two animals folklore associates with the Wild Hunt. In the Maine region, the Chassennquin (another term for the Mesnie Hellequin) is composed of shrieking, invisible night birds. In Upper Brittany, the Menée Anquine includes carnivores that hunt and slay domestic animals.

In order to clearly grasp this figure of the guide of souls (or psychopomp) and warrior hunter, we must return in the calendar, specifically to the date of December 1, via the testimony of an eleventh-century Latin text.

The Blacksmith Monk

The Song in Honor of King Robert (*Carmen ad Rotbertum regem*) is a manuscript written by Adalberon, bishop of Laon, in the first third of the eleventh century.[9] The text is a dialogue between King Robert II (who reigned from 996 to 1031) and Bishop Adalberon himself, a debate focusing on public affairs, beginning with a general illustration of the revolutions that affected the Church and the state. This is followed by a satire on monastic (specifically Clunisian) mores, then by an examination of the ecclesiastical hierarchy and the different castes of society. It ends with a plan of reform that is, in fact, characterized by counter-reform intended to fight the perverse effects of new ideas. Throughout this dialogue, Adalberon expresses extremely conservative positions, whereas the king appears to have been won over to the new ideas. Throughout, the bishop endeavors to return the king to the path of tradition and conservatism without moderating a whit his attacks against the mad reformers, such as Odilon, the famous abbot of Cluny.

In the text we can read a curious portrait of the would-be reformers of the Cluny monastery intended to ridicule the life led within the great Benedictine abbey. "A picture of mores and nothing more, and not precise facts, writes a commentator of the three-day battle waged by the Clunisian militia around December 1 against the Saracens that have invaded the Tours diocese. This is pure burlesque; the casual nature of the story confirms it." Of course, in reading this text, we should be wary of overly categorical judgments.

If we read further in the text, we can see that the satire uses details that come from what we know as carnivalesque folklore, and their insertion in an extremely serious debate should not be cause to overlook their distinctive nature. So let us carefully read over the subsequent portrait of the Cluny monk:

> He wore a large bonnet made of Libyan bear skin. His trailing robe was now pulled halfway up his legs; it was split up the front, nor did it cover his behind. He had strapped around his waist an embroidered baldric, tied as tight as it could possibly be; hanging from his belt was a quantity of the most diverse objects: a bow with its quiver, a hammer and tongs, a sword, a flint, iron for striking it, oak branches to be set aflame. Pants clung to his legs, stretched the length of them. He was skipping and hopping.

The monk, who had been sent on a mission to Cluny, presents himself to his former bishop as a soldier under the orders of Odilon, "king [*sic!*] of Cluny." The bishop then reveals to his former monk a situation of concern: "The Saracens, that race of the most savage mores, has invaded the kingdom of France, sword in hand. They occupy it entirely and are eating away at everything that feeds the soil of Gaul. Everywhere vermilion blood moistens and reddens this earth and swells the torrents that are overflowing from this excess carnage."

This is the eleventh century, and of course the appearance of the Saracens in Gaul, especially in Touraine, at the heart of the kingdom, has no historical foundation. As has been noted by other modern scholars of this text, the Saracen invasions were long since over by this time, and the term Saraceni is probably used metaphorically by Aldalberon to designate another category of people. But which people? ·

To resolve this mystery of the Saracens, we need to pay heed to the date of the battle: "All of this took place, know this well, on the first day of December, but we will again engage in combat during the calends of March." The mention of the calends of December and March allows us to better grasp the meaning of the curious outfit of the monk as well as this apparently mock battle whose true purpose is a carnivalesque release. We should concentrate on the value of these dates for the moment.

Saint Eligius and the Fire of December

December 1 was the feast day of Saint Eligius, a councilor for Clotaire II and Dagobert. An odd exploit is attributed to him in his legend: He was said to have crafted one throne from the gold provided him by King Clotaire and another from the gold that was left over from the creation of the first. Thus the saint who is celebrated during the December calends is a goldsmith and a blacksmith—a specialist in working metal.

It so happens that the costume of the monk described in *The Song in Honor of King Robert* includes a tools familiar to smiths: a hammer and tongs, a flint, iron for striking, and an oak branch for the fire. We cannot overlook that Saint Eligius, commemorated on December 1, was specifically a protector of horses. According to legend, he owned a fairly distinctive horse. In addition, it was said that he could rejuvenate himself by exposing himself to the fire of his forge, which harkens to a very old folklore theme in which Mircea Eliade sees the souvenir of a "mythical-ritual scenario where fires plays a part in an initiatory ordeal."[10] Thus Saint Eligius could be said to be an initiatory master of fire.

A great many toponyms in France come from the ancient name Equaranda. Beneath this name we can recognize a horselike deity comparable to Epona, which was Christianized most likely through the cult of Eligius. Georges Dumézil has shown that in the same way as animals such as the bear and the wolf, the horse was perfectly integrated into the rituals of the Twelve Days separating Christmas and Epiphany and including the changing of the year during the calends of January. In Carinthie,* the equine game practiced in the eleventh century consisted

---

*[Carinthie refers to southern Austria. —*Trans.*]

of smiths with blackened faces attempting to shoe a horse. According to certain traditions, the phantom horse, accompanied by Odin and the band of the furious hunt (Wildes Heer), came to blacksmiths to be shod. The blacksmith monks of whom Adalberon speaks refer to this same tradition. Mircea Eliade reminds us that the blacksmith was connected to initiatory scenarios in male societies.[11] It is probably to this entire ritual group that the disguise of the Cluny monk refers. The master of the forge fire is here joined with the legendary figure of the diabolical sorcerer and the mythical figure of the shaman, who mediates with the Beyond.

The traditions of the December fire are quite ancient; indeed, they were not foreign to ancient Rome. In fact, the month was placed under the protection of Saturn, god of time, and Vesta, goddess of the domestic hearth. Maintained in her honor was a fire, never extinguished, that was lit in temples and in the first room of each house (hence the word *vestibule* for this entrance room). Other fire traditions extend from this during this month: Traditionally, the Yule log must burn at least three days (hence its name *tréfeu*, "three fire," in Brittany).

Likewise, the festivals honoring Saturn are quite well known: the Saturnalia, during which people indulged in all manner of festivities that could verge on the crude. The Saturnalia are usually viewed as the original form of Carnival. Interestingly, during the Middle Ages there was celebrated a kind of Saturnius or Saturnin on November 29, the day before the eve of Saint Eligius's Day (we can note the name's relationship to Saturn). This journey backward in the calendar is necessary because the Celtic festivals took place over three consecutive nights. Furthermore, Adalberon's text specifies that the battle lasted three days.* We thus find ourselves in the presence of a new and discreet mythological survival.

We can thus conclude that the disguise of the blacksmith monk is not presented merely to be facetious or comic. It is in fact connected to

---

*[Saturnalia was a weeklong celebration that occurred during what is now Christmas, a month later than the November 29 celebration, which occurred over three days, not seven. —*Trans.*]

ritual elements present in an old calendar myth in which we find the simultaneous appearance of the mythic blacksmith, the magical horse, and the rites associated with the reversal of time marked by the solstice. A popular song offers a strongly relevant reminder that Saint Eligius restores everything to its place. This restoration assured by the saint can also be understood in terms of the calendar. During the Middle Ages, there were two Saint Eligius festivals at two essential times of the year: December 1 (near the winter solstice) and June 25 (near the summer solstice). By supervising the solstice, Saint Eligius assisted at the reversal of the cosmos and ensured his own brilliant blossoming.

December 6, Saint Nicholas's Day

According to legend, Aubert de Varangéville brought back from the Crusades a phalange of one of Saint Nicholas's fingers. This relic drew numerous pilgrims to Lorraine, to Saint-Nicolas-de-Port, near Nancy. The miraculous finger fits into an entire framework of ancient beliefs that certain names connected to Nicholas allow us to unearth.

Nicholas was a bishop of Myra (Myre) in Asia Minor. Interestingly, in old French *mire* means both medicine and doctor, which can explain the devotion that grew around this thaumaturge saint. While all saints are, in fact, miracle workers, the relic of Nicholas's finger possesses a remarkable distinguishing feature: According to Tobler-Lommatzch's *Dictionary of Old French*, the finger commonly known as the ring finger is, in medieval French, the *doit mire*,[12] an old name by all accounts, considering that the Latin author Macrobius speaks of a *digitus medicinalis*.[13] Given that the healing relic of the bishop of Myra was a saint's finger, it can be presumed to have been this *doit mire*.

In addition to his gifts as a healer, Nicholas was an excellent magician. This good phantom saved people who called upon his aid and sometimes brought them gifts (such as the money offered to three young girls who were in danger of becoming prostitutes because their families were in need). This gift giving is a trait preserved by the mythical Santa Claus,[14] who flies through the air on a sleigh pulled by reindeer. As we have said, Santa Claus's aerial vehicle is clearly related to the parade of revenants mentioned in the many tales concerning the Wild Hunt. The folklore of Santa Claus (who became Father Christmas) pushes to the forefront Saint Nicholas's connection to the Otherworld. Indeed, Nicholas is a genie of passage. The distributor of abundance and the guarantor of fertility, much like other saints of the same period (Saint Martin, for example), he owns a secret connection with celestial and underground riches.

In truth, Nicholas has a strong connection to the subterranean world. The element nickel was discovered in 1751 and was given an abbreviation of the name Nicholas. A mischievous goblin also shares a name with the saint. In mythology, goblins (like dwarves) are connected both to the world underground and to its mineral wealth. In fact, the German word *Kupfernickel* meant "copper goblin" before it became the name of the element. Another form of wealth from beneath the ground is salt. The first site where the worship of Saint Nicholas was established in France is Saint-Nicolas-de-Port, next to Varangéville, since the Middle Ages an important Lorraine site for the extraction of salt. As if to remind people of this bond between Nicholas and salt, the church of Varangéville remains dedicated to Saint Gorgon, a martyr whose torturers salted his intestines. Saint Gorgon of Varangéville irresistibly brings to mind the Gargantua of Rabelais, whose connection to salt is well recounted in the novel. The most famous alchemist of the Middle Ages was named Nicholas Flamel. Perhaps Saint Nicholas prompted him to seek initiation into the secrets of chemistry.

According to *The Golden Legend,* to win revenge on Nicholas, who had broken her statue, Diana disguised herself as a nun and gave to sailors returning to the saint's home a highly combustible oil intended to destroy the sanctuary where Nicholas preached. Nicholas appeared to the sailors and had them burn this oil while still at sea, thus disarming this malevolent trap. Diana's magic oil (might this have been the first appearance of petroleum in the Middle Ages?) was thereby neutralized by the saint who deployed a (Christian) magic that was stronger than that of the pagan goddess. Behind this pagan deity Diana, Dea Ana of

Fig. 3.1. A depiction of
Saint Nicholas

Fig. 3.2. A representation of
Saint Gorgon

the Celts, we can see the great goddess, protector of smiths, bards, and doctors.

The essential piece of pagan memory related to Saint Nicholas concerns the figure of Père Fouettard, who regularly accompanies the saint on all his visits to children in Alsace, Lorraine, northern France, and Luxembourg. Père Fouettard* is a bogeyman, a true Wild Man and hairy ghost with a red beard. In contemporary folklore, he is the fossilized witness of the saint's pagan ancestor. Fouettard's appearance brings to mind that of all the Wild Men of Carnival. Half man and half beast, he embodies the primitive world, though in fact he belongs to the Otherworld and is one of its masters. He is the fairy ogre, a master of abundance and wealth and a Plutonian god of the dead, but is dispossessed of these positive features in his new status as follower of the saintly bishop, who lords over him. Saint Nicholas drags him along just as other saints do the monster, or tarrasque, they have tamed.

Saint Nicholas confirms his pagan ancestor's aspect of abundance.

---

*[Roughly translated, Père Fouettard means "father spanker."—*Trans.*]

In Siberia, Mikoula is a god of both harvests and the beer that is linked to drunkenness. The Russian verb *nicolitsja* means to "get intoxicated." As part of the posterity of Mikoula, Nicholas and subsequently Santa Claus have become carnivalesque figures who distribute abundance during the heart of winter.

The Christmas Spruce Tree, Pine Tree, and Hawthorn (*Arbutus*)

The smith's fire of December is fed by certain trees. Among the immemorial rites of Christmas, the decorated spruce tree figures most prominently. The custom of decorating the spruce comes from Alsace, where the first incontestable testimonies on the rite of the Christmas spruce date from the sixteenth century. The account books for the town of Selestat on December 21, 1521, mention an expenditure of two shillings as pay for the forest guard members responsible for surveillance of the woods that surrounded the town. This is a clue pointing to the fact that already at this time the true infatuation of families for the forest king was usually accompanied by the looting of certain forests owned by the domain. A 1419 document from the municipal archives of Fribourg, in Germany, confirms this custom. In addition, since the Middle Ages people have hung spruce branches called *Weihnachtsmeyen,* equivalent to Christmas boughs, at this time of year. There was also a well-known custom of raising spruce trees decorated with red apples on the parvis of Rhenish churches, which were said to commemorate the fall of Adam and Eve. Here again biblical allegory merges with a rite of pagan origin, which is no surprise, especially in this instance: The tree of the world of Faery became the tree of the earthly Paradise. With its foliage that remains green even during the cold season, the spruce tree naturally became a symbol of immortality, perennial nature, and the Nativity of the Savior.

The spruce is one of many in the large family of spiny trees or bramble bushes around which have gravitated numerous legends sharing a common origin in a great myth. The rites of Christmas related to such plants can be understood fully only in light of the rites of May that enhance the value of plants and trees. Weihnachtsmeyen can be translated fairly literally as the May of Christmas. In fact, the custom of Christmas reproduces the rites of May 1 that consist of planting trees in front of certain houses.

Generally speaking, the worship of trees was particularly hardy in the West before the coming of Christianity. One episode in Saint Martin's life as told by Sulpicius Severus provides particular corroboration of the substantial worship of the pine tree in Celtic society: Martin had just destroyed an old, impious temple without encountering any resistance. Yet when he sought to uproot a pine tree dedicated to a local deity, the pagans initially opposed his efforts, then suggested a kind of bargain. They said, "If you have trust in your god, remain under that tree while we cut it down." Martin accepted and was bound beneath the tree on the side toward which it was already leaning. When the tree was at the point of falling, Martin made the sign of the cross. Instead of collapsing on him, the pine fell in the opposite direction, just missing the pagans. With supreme skill, the Christian text clearly mentions the mythic pagan role played by the pine before diverting to the Christian God the magic power attributed to this tree by the pagans.

In England, the hawthorn is considered to be the ancestor of the Christmas tree. A pious legend explains the notoriety enjoyed by this shrub: Joseph of Arimathea, who had taken the body of Christ following the Crucifixion, was said to have ended up in Glastonbury, England, a major site in the Arthurian legend. According to legend, he planted his staff in the soil on Christmas Eve, and subsequently a flowering hawthorn immediately grew on the spot. Until around the sixteenth century the English offered each other as a Christmas gift a branch of the Glastonbury hawthorn that had allegedly grown from the staff of Joseph of Arimathea. It was said that it always flowered on Christmas Eve.

In a thirteenth-century French romance entitled *Durmart le Gallois* (Durmart the Welshman) there appears a magic tree, sparkling with tiny flames, which a knight recognizes as a manifestation from the Land of Faery. Here we find the otherworldly will-o'-the-wisps associated with a sacred tree. The motif of the illuminated tree appears on other occasions in medieval literature, confirming the existence of a Celtic myth of thorn trees that has left traces in French place-names such as Epinay, Epinal, and so on,* as well as in several pious legends.

The thorn of Evron (in Mayenne) confirms the magical value of the hawthorn in Celtic tradition. Behind the high altar of the church of Evron there is a highly artistic representation of a tree trunk, which takes the form of a pyramid with thornlike branches that appear to grow from it. At one time a statue of the Virgin was placed in a niche at the bottom of the trunk. A local legend explains why this site was made sacred: During the seventh century, a pilgrim passing through Evron was carrying a relic of the Virgin he brought back from the Holy Land. Because he was near collapse from fatigue, he sought to rest near a spring, hanging his reliquary in some nearby bushes. While he slept, however, the hawthorn bushes started growing out of all proportion and lifted the reliquary high off the ground. It was through this miracle, the legend concludes, that the Virgin let it be known that she wanted to be honored at this site.

The founding of the church of Varangéville in Meuthe-et-Moselle is explained by a similar legend. During the seventh century, Pope Paul I gave relics of Saint Gorgon to Saint Chrodegang, bishop of Metz and founder of Gorze Abbey in Moselle. Chrodegang repatriated them immediately into Lorraine, leading a procession that soon found itself close to Varangéville when nightfall forced them to halt. The reliquary was hung from a thornbush for safekeeping during the night, but the next morning all could see that the bush had inexplicably grown, moving the reliquary out of reach. This miracle was interpreted as a sign from heaven, and a church dedicated to Saint Gorgon was immediately constructed on the site.

Taking literally these pious legends about the hawthorn would be both naive and fruitless. Viewing them as the fossilized testimonies of old pagan myths seems much more in keeping with their strangeness. In any case, such legends cast a decisive light on the profane origin of our Christmas tree.

---

*[*Epine* is the French word for "thorn."—*Trans.*]

Analysis of the rites of Christmas has revealed it to be particularly fertile ground for understanding the myths and mysteries of this period. Again, it is necessary to have at our disposal the texts that give the language of the rites its profound consistency. Christmas clearly belongs to an enchanted time that allows the Otherworld to break into and enter the human world. The Christian translation of this set of myths allows the archaic memory that orients this holiday to poke through to the surface. In truth, Christianity extended paganism by introducing another kind of logic into the pagan elements it preserved or by scattering the exploded symbols of myth over the wheel of Time.

FOUR

February 1, Imbolc

Fat Sunday, coupled this time with Candlemas, started off these brief Saturnalia that would be, at the least, as complete as those of Rome. We have recalled the souvenirs of antiquity in this regard; we have endeavored to explain this strange holiday that returns to our Christian civilization the souvenirs of the pagan world . . . Everyone has translated this fact to their liking: Some find in it a symbol of abolished superstitions, which is held up for public ridicule by the victorious cult; some see in the procession of the fattest steer of the year the glorification of agricultural labor; others finally have credited its existence to religious tolerance that, at the entry into a strict Lent, allows the flesh to gather its strength and to have done with joy before entering into penitence. The Phalansterian journal* has inveighed against the spirit of the bizarre masquerade that accompanies the fatted bull and wonders if it would not be more worthy and logical to give a completely agricultural character to this festival and to display around the bull, instead of bizarrely equipped masqueraders, the ranchers, farmers, or stock breeders who would have provided the nation with this enormous lot of steaks and sirloins.

We cannot be too sorry to see opinion go astray in this way.

---

*[Phalansterian refers to the Utopian vision of French visionary Charles Fourier, whose vision of an ideal society included social divisions he called Phalansteries. —*Trans.*]

The procession of the fatted bull is not an agricultural festival, but
a religious, historical, and, so to speak, mystical ceremony.
                    GÉRARD DE NERVAL, *L'ARTISTE*, FEBRUARY 8, 1845

The eight carnivalesque dates that give rhythm to the annual calendar correspond to a pre-Christian cycle of movable feasts that depend on the lunar phases. These feasts, however, have undergone a more or less marked Christianization by virtue of being fixed to specific periods in the calendar. In other words, these feasts, originally movable because they were tied to lunar cycles, have been fixed to set days as they have been integrated into the Christian calendar. In February or midwinter these include Candlemas (February 2), Saint Brigid's Day (February 1), the feast of Saint-Ours of Aosta (also February 1), Saint Blaise's Day (February 3), and so forth. Thanks to still living folklore testimonies, some of these dates allow us to guess the importance of the ancient mythical mechanisms they supplanted. Best known among these are the rites of Mardi Gras. Oddly enough, this festival was never fixed to a set date, no doubt because it remained quite vital and by nature quite rebellious toward Christianity. It is during this period of the calendar that the great carnivals of the entire world still take place today.

The Celtic holiday of February 1, in theory the closest to Mardi Gras, was known as Imbolc,[1] which commemorates the moment of the year when the sheep began to give milk again. In the medieval calendar, the ritual function of this festival was important because it provided the junction between the cycle of Christmas (a fixed holiday) and the cycle of Carnival-Lent, which moves in the calendar according to the moon's phases. The commemorations surrounding Imbolc enable us to penetrate the major arcanum of Carnival.

Masks

Masquerades and disguises are among our first associations with Mardi Gras.[2] Indeed, the mask is the obligatory companion to this festival. To truly grasp the significance of this costume piece, we must refer to Walter von Wartburg's scholarly study of this word in his *Etymological Dictionary of French*.[3] The root of the word *mask* seems to be pre–Indo-European, designating the spirits and creatures of the Otherworld who reveal themselves to humans at certain times of the year.

We find eleventh-century corroboration of the word *mask* in the Latin *talamasca*. In the text that mentions this term, Hincmar, the bishop of Reims, condemns the disguises used at masquerades in the company of bears:

> May he [the Christian] avoid the noisy displays of joy and vulgar laughter, may he neither tell nor sing useless stories, may he not consent that in his presence others indulge in the obscene games of the bear; may he not on that occasion wear the masks of demons that the vulgar call *talamasca* because these involve diabolical practices condemned by the canons of the Church.[4]

These masquerades no doubt involved ritual customs in which the belief in ghosts was combined with spectacular or grotesque dances. The Carnival-like parades found almost everywhere in Eurasia are organized around this traditional core. In fact, the pagan customs stigmatized by the archbishop do not arise merely from the simple amusements that stage the vulgar displays of bear leaders. Instead, they involve pagan customs he prudishly describes as "obscene games" in which individuals that are disguised and associated with bears go under the name *talamasca*. These probably participated in a facetious masquerade, complete with dances and mimicry, which we might best envision from our modern bear festivals, such as the one held in Prats-de-Mollo in the Catalonian Pyrenees.[5] Indeed, the traditional farces of Carnival include men disguised as bears who smear with soot the faces of those they catch—that is, the bears craft for their victims a black mask that carries them back into the world of the revenants.[6]

Hincmar doesn't specify the exact dates of the ritual parades during which these bears make their appearance, but he does condemn them vigorously—proof that they come from a set of pre-Christian beliefs and superstitions involving the worship of revenants and relations with the Beyond that Christianity attempted to fight. In fact, in Hincmar's description we find ourselves once again in the presence of an authentic manifestation of that Wild Man whose mythic importance we have already assessed. The element of masks suggests that these revels involved revenants and that they were in some way connected to funerary cults. Interestingly, Claude Lecouteux has noted that "the laws frequently state that *masca* is the vulgar name for the *striges,* and Gervase of Tilbury[7] wrote around 1210 that *mask* is the vulgar and Gallic name for *lamia.*"* Carnival was thus presented as a festival of the intrusion of revenants, the moment when the beings of the Otherworld came to mingle among humans for a time.

February 14, Saint Valentine's Day

As we saw earlier, though we cannot prove any direct connection, the name Carna is reminiscent of Carnival. Indeed, both names reflect a much older tradition shared by the majority of Indo-European or, more accurately, Eurasian peoples.

Let us look more closely at the final syllable *val* of Carnival. We might note first that, mythically and onomastically speaking, it is certainly present in Arthurian literature at the end of names such as Lanval and Perceval. We can also note that *val* is directly linked to the syllable *gal,* if we take into account the phonetic evolution of the guttural in Romanesque languages. A hagionym such as Saint Gall and related French place-names such as Saint-Gal (in Lozère), Saint-Gal-sur-Sioule (in Puy-de-Dôme), Saint Gall (in the lower Rhine), and Saint-Romain-en-Gall (in Rhône) offer evidence of the existence of pre-Christian mythical and legendary substrata revolving around these *gal* or, by extension, *val.* Furthermore, all these place-names offer a significant geographical allocation over the whole of French territory. In addition, some designate sites that are known for their archaeological remains from the Gallo-

---

*[Lamia are Latin forms of a female vampire who particularly fed on poets. —*Trans.*]

Roman and Celtic periods (Saint-Romain-en-Gall near Vienne in Isère, for example), while others have decidedly Christian associations (such as the Abbey of Saint Gall in Switzerland, which was a very important monastic establishment during the early Middle Ages).[8] The word *gal* most likely belongs to the pre-Christian memory of the West and might refer to rites and beliefs to which Carnival still testifies.

We know that medieval hagiography has preserved many of these pre-Christian religious substrata. In order to reappropriate ancient beliefs, the Church invented the figures of saints—both men and women—who both borrowed the names of their pagan predecessors and possessed mythical attributes similar to those of their pagan models. This is why we cannot be surprised at worship devoted today to certain mysterious saints—including Saint Valentine. In fact, along with the time of year of his celebration, the initial syllable of his name—*val*—compels us to establish a potential link with the mythology of Carnival.

With a commemoration date of February 14, the feast day of Saint Valentine is perhaps not accidentally set in the period of Carnival. The principle reasoning that saints are celebrated on the anniversary date of their death is hardly defensible once we have devoted ourselves to a historical analysis of the calendar. It is rather more likely that the saints are

Fig. 4.1. Saint Valentine

the successors to pre-Christian pagan deities connected to certain times of the year and that each preserves a part of a deity's aura and mythical functions. In other words, the imaginal substance of a saint is composed of a subtle blend of paganism and Christianity. From this point of view, the worship of saints seeks to absorb the polytheistic tendencies of the pre-Christian religion into the monotheistic framework of Christianity.

It is curious that February 14 is celebrated in five regions to commemorate no fewer than five distinct saints all bearing the name Valentine. This could be viewed as simply a banal phenomenon of hagiographic competition, with each region claiming the authenticity of the "true" Saint Valentine. More revealing is the fact that there was obviously a specific need to occupy this date of February 14 with a saint bearing the name Valentine. This phenomenon points to the camouflaging of paganism—most specifically, the rites and myths commemorated on this date in the pagan calendar—in several regions. These five Valentines of February 14 are:

- A priest of Rome who was allegedly martyred on the Flaminian Way in the year 270
- A bishop martyr of Terni, Italy
- A bishop of Toro, Spain
- A confessor honored in Puy
- A martyr in Africa

The simultaneity of these commemorations cannot be the result of simple coincidence. There had to have been a good reason to restore to the carnivalesque date of February 14 one or more saints with a name that includes the syllable *val.* Perhaps the answer can be found in the existence of a pagan deity whose name or nickname contains the same syllable. We might find a clue to the convergence of the pagan and Christian figures in a major episode with mythical connotations that has been well preserved by the Hindu tradition. Here we might take the first step toward an Indo-European origin for Carnival.

The Ritual Death of the Giant

We find the same myth in both the context of Carnival and the legend of Saint Valentine: death by decapitation of a divine figure. The martyr Valentine was decapitated just like the giant of Carnival. This rite of decapitation, which incidentally refers back to a cultural practice well known to the Celts, can be found in the Rig Veda, in which it is associated with a deity who hears the explicit name of Karna. This Hindu deity subsequently suffers a ritual decapitation inscribed within the context of the seasons, thereby offering an explanation of the infinite cycle:

> The head falls first, then the body collapses . . . Like the sun that has reached the middle of the autumn sky, the head falls to the ground in front of the army, like the red-disked sun from the mountain as it sets . . . The decapitated head of Karna shines like the globe of the sun as it departs the sky . . . The head of Karna falls upon the earth like the star with a thousand rays at the end of the day.

This text, incorporating Karna into the sun, reproduces the drama of the sun, which each year grows and shrinks in the sky. The legend of Karna thereby appears as a cosmogonic myth whose seasonal nature echoes the liturgies of Carnival. When we recognize the importance of the seasonal character of Carnival customs, there is no room for surprise at this cosmic reference. The myth sheds light on the meaning of the rite and vice versa.

In medieval and contemporary folklore, Carnival ends with the death of the giant king, who is sacrificed in a bonfire on Mardi Gras evening. In many regions a mannequin clad in rags plays the role of the fat Carnival giant. After a sham trial, he is condemned to be either tossed into the flames or decapitated or even drowned, after which the half-starved king of Lent arrives to replace him for forty days.

The medieval romance *La Manekine* recounts certain rites of the medieval Carnival and dates them in accordance with the annual calendar. Interestingly, these rites of the Middle Ages display very little difference from those of modern Carnival. Among them we find that of the mannequin destined to be burned the first Sunday of Lent (Firebrand Sunday). These rites of both medieval times and the present were in some cases much older than the Middle Ages, if we can take Julius Caesar at his word when he mentions similar sacrificial practices among the Gauls. Furthermore, this giant of Carnival cannot help but bring to mind the gigantic figure of Gargantua, which provides further corroboration of the long medieval tradition surrounding him.

Yet a medieval romance does supply proof of the existence before Rabelais of a gigantic figure bearing the name of Gargan. The romance *Florimont,* written in 1188 by Aymon de Varennes, presents a giant named Garganeüs who is fought and beheaded by a young hero in quest of a kingdom.[9] Folklorists' ignorance of medieval texts has led more than one to deny the existence of a Carnival myth centered on the figure of a giant, yet it is undeniable that the myth of the giant of Carnival exists and that this giant appears in the rites in varied but perfectly recognizable shapes every forty days. Finally, the meaning of this myth can be clarified by the rites practiced on these same carnivalesque dates and in those medieval texts that often explicitly depict this gigantic figure.

It is striking to see the syllable *val,* as in the word Carnival, lead, by way of the intermediary figure of Valentine, toward the ritual decapitation of the Vedic Karna, who himself shares an onomastic relationship with the Italian goddess of beans, Carna. And we cannot forget that Carna contains the first two syllables of the word Carnival.* Such convergences are more than striking, even though they should not lead to the commingling of the traditions they compare. Again, we must look most closely at the Indo-European kinships and analogies that are in question.

Of course the etymon of the word Carnival remains a mystery, but the light shed by the pagan liturgies of February could provide an explanation. In any case, such mythological, ritual, and calendrical convergences reinforce the notion that Carnival is the folklorized form of

---

*[Carnival is Carnaval in French, making the relationship of the festival to the goddess even more explicit. —*Trans.*]

an old Indo-European religion. Given this, the open conflict that was entertained between these true pre–Indo-European rites and Christianity throughout the Middle Ages and far beyond should be little cause for surprise.

February 1, Saint Brigid's Day

Saint Brigid of Kildare, the great Celtic "goddess," figures among the Celtic deities who were Christianized into saints through the efforts of Irish monks. In the medieval calendar, she is commemorated on February 1, the eve of Candlemas, forty days after Christmas. This privileged position in the calendar confers upon her an eminent mythical value. Brigid was, in fact, the Christianized figure of the mother goddess of the Celts—that is to say, the sole female figure of the Celtic pantheon who was simultaneously the mother, wife, and daughter of the male gods.

Upon close examination, the golden legend of Saint Brigid is rich with marvelous tales involving birds and other flying creatures. In fact, Saint Brigid was credited with magically creating a bird to console a young girl after she lost a small silver chain.[10] Like Brigid, the abbesses of Kildare, still according to legend, resurrected birds that had been roasted and eaten by arranging their bones in a certain order.[11] The same miracle is attributed to other saints (both French and English), all of which harkens back to a common model that has a liturgical commemoration in the calendar of Carnival (generally in February). Thus we recall the similar motif of the resurrected roasted chicken in certain hagiographic traditions such as that of Saint James of Compostela, which likewise looks to an older motif connected to the Celtic demiurge, the deity ruling life and death, the great goddess or her consort who is capable of resuscitating the corpses of both humans and animals. Indeed, Saint Germain d'Auxerre, celebrated at another key period of the calendar (July 31), resurrects a calf from the animal's bones, as does the Germanic god Thor. Claude Lecouteux judiciously sees the vestiges of shamanic rites in such actions,[12] and it is perfectly plausible that these Germanic myths infiltrated the beliefs of the Celtic world.

Celtic mythology does in fact have bird-goddesses who did not vanish with the Celts. Quite the contrary, they survived the decline of Celtic religion and metamorphosed with Christianity. It is generally little known that the ancient Celtic goddesses possessed the gift of being able to transform into birds. The great bird-goddess Morgan, or Morgana, who is both many and one, is the incarnation of warrior sovereignty.[13] Similar to the German Valkyrie, she is the one who selects and summons the valorous warrior who will live with her in the Otherworld.

All that the Middle Ages preserved of these bird-goddesses were saints with one goose foot. The Church either has minimized the importance of these odd female figures or has simply relegated them to anonymity. It no doubt deemed it indecent to exhibit these superstitions of another age, yet it still saw fit to insert into the calendar a female saint named Neomaye (or Neomaise) who had one goose foot, as if to exorcise the superstitions associated with the pre-Christian form of this saint. There is no doubt that Saint Neomaye has been worshipped only since the fifteenth or sixteenth century (no earlier evidence of her cult has been found), but the earlier existence of a related mythic pagan figure is not at all subject to doubt.

The *Life of Saint Enimie* by Bertrand de Marseille, dating from the thirteenth century, involves an adaptation into the Provençal language of a much older Latin text and represents a popular version of this myth.[14] Although Enimie does not possess any specific feature relating her to a bird, her true nature forms a solid connection with the bird-women of Celtic myth. We can verify this through a simple comparison of the stories of Enimie and Neomaye. Both these young women were confronted with the problem of an imposed marriage, being forced against their will to marry men they neither knew nor loved. Each requested either an affliction that would make them undesirable (leprosy in the case of Enimie and a goose's foot in the case of Neomaye) or transformation into a bird. The goose's foot is an obvious ancient sign of transformation in accordance with the goddess nature. One of the oldest of all French literary texts, the *Séquence de sainte Eulalie*, recounts the tale of a young girl whom the king attempts to rape being miraculously transformed into a dove.[15] This dove* is reminiscent of the numerous Saint Colombes in place-names that were spread throughout France. Behind these Saint Colombes is the descendant of an ancient bird-goddess of the Celts, which folklore managed to recycle in this way.

The Breton writer François-René de Chateaubriand carried the memory of this myth in his *Memoires d'Outre-Tombe* (Memoirs from Beyond the Grave),[16] in which he recounts "the true story of a wild duck, in the town of Monfort-la-Cane-les-Saint-Mâlo," a story his mother told to him when he was still a child. According to this tale, in order to escape her being raped, Saint Nicholas transforms a young girl into a duck. She is said to return every year on May 9 (the commemoration of the return of the saint's remains to Bari) to haunt the site of her providential transformation:

> *A duck the beauty had become*
> *And flew off through a grate*
> *Into a pond full of lentils.*

Saint Vincent

There exist several martyrs by the name of Vincent who are commemorated on different dates of the year and who possess features that give them distinct identities. The index of the *Vies des saints et bienheureux* (Lives of the Saints and the Blessed) established by the Benedictines of Paris provides the following inventory of Vincents:

- An African martyr and companion of Datif (January 27)
- A martyr of the third or fourth century in Agen (June 9)
- A martyr from Avila who was accompanied by Sabine and Christète (October 27)
- A martyr from Collioure who died around 303 (April 19)
- A man martyred in Spain on an unknown date in the company of Lieda (September 1)

---

*[The word *dove* is *colombe* in French. —*Trans.*]

- A man martyred in Gerona sometime near 304 in the company of Victor and Oronce (January 22)
- A martyr from Porto killed on an unknown date (May 24)
- Three men martyred in Rome, one on the Appian Way (August 6), another on the Aurelian Way (August 25), and the last on the Tibertine Way (July 24)
- The martyr of Valencia, perhaps most important (January 22)

These different Vincents quite certainly are related to the same model whose origin is to be found in a mythic figure of paganism. The most remarkable examples issued from this prototype would seem to be the martyr of Valencia in Spain and the martyr of Gerona (both January 22). As for the three Roman Vincents, all celebrated within a month (July 24 to August 25) and, with respect to the first one, on the eve of the feast day of James the Greater, also known as Saint James of Compostela, these appear to be triplets of the earlier figure. We can immediately note the calendrical symmetry of these two series of commemorations (January 22 and the month between July 24 and August 25), for they are separated by a six-month interval and are placed in the two extreme seasons of the year.

Since 1235 the Vincent adopted by Lisbon as its protector has been honored in the Agen region under the name of Saint Vincent of the Ravens. This designation alludes to a mishap that almost befell the martyr's corpse. After having been tossed into a pasture and left for wild animals, the saint's cadaver was allegedly guarded by ravens, who kept watch over the body's integrity and drove off a wolf that sought to devour it. According to the legend, Vincent's remains were then sewn up in a sack to which a millstone was attached. When it was thrown into the open sea, the sack floated and was tossed back onto shore, where Christians found it and shrouded the corpse.

In the twelfth century, following the Saracen invasions, Vincent's relics were discovered on the side of the Algarves in a place known as Promontorium Sacrum. This site had already been deemed sacred in ancient times, for there the Romans had erected a temple to Hercules. Strabo

Fig. 4.2. Saint Vincent

gives the Celtic name for this site: Port of the Two Ravens. Miraculously, the relics abandoned on a ship after the saint's martyrdom landed near Lisbon, where there already stood a church dedicated to Saint Justa and Saint Rufina, the patron saints of Seville. Since the arrival of Vincent's relics, however, the coat of arms for the city of Lisbon bears the boat that brought to its walls the corpse of the honored martyr.

There is no lack of evidence contradicting what appears from the outset to be both a pious and an incoherent invention. The relics of Saint Vincent are said to have been held since the ninth century at the Saint-Benoît de Castres Abbey, which would have necessitated a double theft enacted first in Valencia, then in Saragossa. Of course, both these Spanish cities claim to have preserved the integrity of their martyr's body and reject as pure fabrication the story of its removal to Castres. In any event, other relics of the saint are said to exist throughout France, in Auvergne, Alsace, Lorraine, Champagne, and Dauphiné. If we were to gather together all these relics and reassemble the body of the saint, no doubt they would form a very strange skeleton with an abnormal number of fingers and arms!

In fact, rather than peremptorily stake out a position on the authority of this or that site, or even on the historicity of the martyr himself, it is more important to question the network of pre-Christian beliefs that the Church strove to conceal beneath Vincent. By all evidence, this saint played in France and Portugal the same role Patrick played in Ireland. By inserting them within a Christian context, he borrowed the great sacred themes of Celtic mythology: the inviolability of the sacred body and the divination and divinity of birds.

According to Celtic mythology, the druid-god magically masters fire and water; through incantations he can stave off the danger these two elements represent when someone tries to burn him or drown him. The tales of certain "deaths" of divine or semidivine figures as they are told in Celtic texts (Irish and Welsh) of the Middle Ages invariably bring to mind the Christian martyrs. The martyr inherits all the magical gifts of the druid—whether he is drawn and quartered, drowned, or burned, he displays his complete invulnerability.

The abandonment to the waves of a cradle or basket holding either the body of a newborn or a beheaded cadaver—related to the voyage of Vincent's abandoned remains—belongs to the most ancient of mythologies. In his work on the Syrian goddess Lucian, a writer from the first century C.E. reports that a head coming from Egypt arrived by sea in the port of Byblos on the Syrian coast. The legend goes on to say that the coffin carrying the remains of the body of Osiris had been hurled into the sea and was carried by the waves to Byblos. Since that time, this ritual sea voyage was reenacted on an annual basis.

As in the case of Saint Tropez* or Saint Vincent, in this theme of important cargo left to the vagaries of the waves at no time is the boat carrying the holy relic threatened with being swallowed up or destroyed. In his treatise on divination, Cicero recalls that people born during the dog days of the year are guaranteed not to be drowned. Because, as told, it was impossible to drown the corpse of Vincent, we must therefore assume that this saint was born during the hottest part of the year. This canicular birth date (in the sign of Leo) and the commemoration of his

---

*[Little is known about this saint other than that he was martyred by the emperor Nero and the boat carrying his remains landed at what is now St. Tropez, also known as St. Torpes. —*Trans.*]

death in the annual calendar make it possible to rediscover the two axes of time and the two annual crossings of the Milky Way, a true astro-mythological key to the such myths.[17]

We can further note that the cult of Isis and Osiris is also linked to the hot weather, in their case to the season when the Nile floods. For Vincent, his specific connection to the dog days of summer, a period of great change, perhaps explains why he was linked with the mythology of wine (the first syllable of his name cannot help but call to mind this beverage). Saint Vincent has remained the patron saint of vintners to this day.

Now let us turn to the role of the sacred raven in the tradition of Saint Vincent. In Ireland, this bird is the animal metamorphosis of the goddess of war (the name of the raven is Bodb).[18] Furthermore, among the Celts the raven is a sacred animal associated with the legendary founding of certain cities—for example, Lyon (Lugdunum), a noteworthy case because it seems to be a duplicate of Lisbon. In both cases sacred birds designated a site destined for great religious notoriety and, secondarily, political repute.

According to A. H. Knappe, "Bran is the raven guide of sailors and patron of the sea voyaging of the ancient Celts."[19] Given this, the connection of a raven to a saint condemned to a funerary voyage is completely mythic in nature. The numerous superstitions regarding the raven maintain the bird's augural value. In the domain of folklore, a story from the Brothers Grimm entitled *The Seven Ravens* recounts the transformation of a young girl into a raven and offers an invitation to compare this tradition with certain Irish mythological tales featuring the goddess Morgan or Bodb.

In addition, ravens are associated with Saint Apollinaire, whose feast day is celebrated six months after Saint Vincent's Day, on July 23. This day, the founding of an Italian town, a pagan custom whose mythical character is hard to contest, and the birds converge in this legend related by the twelfth-century geographer Giraut de Barri (Giraldus Cambrensis):

In Italy, near the noble city of Ravenna, all kinds of ravens, crows, and jackdaws coming from every region of Italy gather every year on the day of Saint Apollinaire, as if by appointment. By virtue of ancient custom, they are given the corpse of a horse on this day. If you were to ask me the reason, I would not venture to explain it, except, perhaps, to attribute it to a custom established so long ago it has become almost second nature. There, where the body of the saint would have been laid to rest, the birds gather—or rather they are gathered by a miracle performed by this saint. It is this reason, this gathering of the birds, that gives rise to the belief that Ravenna was originally called, in the Teuton's tongue (*teutonica lingua*), Ravensburgh, which means "city of the ravens."[20]

With the regularity of clockwork, the motif of the augural ravens (or, in some variants, roosters) is arranged around the eight major festivals of the pre-Christian calendar. It is the myth of a sea journey that ensures the founding of a city. Like Saint James the Greater (celebrated on July 25) and Saint Vincent of the Ravens (celebrated on January 22), the decapitated body of Saint Tropez (honored on May 17) made its way to shore by virtue of an enchanted barge.

The marvelous ships that sail without a rudder or pilot form a leitmotif in the Celtic imaginal realm. Such vessels are generally associated with certain key dates of the calendar in various literary genres (hagiography, epic texts, the Breton lays, and so forth) and in the romance *La Manekine*. Found in scarcely differing form in various port cities of Europe is a Boullonaise legend that recounts how, during the time of Dagobert, a statue of the Virgin arrived on an uncaptained boat.[21] After having made land, it immediately inspired the devotion of the faithful and was placed in the church of Notre Dame de Boulogne until 1793, when it was destroyed during the Revolution. Is there any historical likelihood that this boat actually arrived? It is difficult to accept, for the event presents itself as legendary, meaning it stems from a story invented to meet the needs of Christianization. Still, we should not reject the belief behind it as unlikely or superstitious. Such medieval beliefs are interesting for what they reveal (or conceal) about an archaic mentality that has not been judged on its own. In fact, the motif of the marvelous ship contains the elements of an old Celtic myth, easily recognizable though camouflaged beneath a Christian surface.

It is connected to the pagan festival of Imbolc (February 1) that appears as a particular commemoration of the great goddess Brigid and which Christianity answered with the Feast of the Purification of the Virgin (February 2), also known as Candlemas. During this holiday, the custom of offering small breads shaped as boats no doubt recalls the mythical, magical sea voyage associated with this date.

A French literary text itself adapted from folklore of Celtic origin enables us to recover certain elements of this motif. This text of pagan origin has a source much older than hagiographic legends. The *Lai de Guigemar,* written by Marie de France in the second half of the twelfth century, recounts a marvelous voyage to the Otherworld made by a young nobleman, Guigemar, sorely wounded in the thigh and transported unknowingly by a strange boat that has no pilot. Instead, the vessel is pulled by a mysterious force that is definitively revealed to be the power of Faery. The ship carries Guigemar toward a fairy, an avatar of the great goddess of the Otherworld. Similarly, in the *Vengeance Raguidel,* an Arthurian romance of the thirteenth century, the corpse of a fairy knight pierced by the shaft of a lance is transported by a magical boat to the knight Gawain, who alone knows how to extract the murderous lance from the knight's body.

The hagiographic narratives of, for example, Saint Tropez and Saint James of Compostella, crafted in large part from Celtic motifs (which we also find in the profane literature of the Middle Ages), have retained the trace of these old, pre-Christian mythological traditions. Among these literary texts of mythical origin presenting this same motif of enchanted seafaring is the legend of the swan knight.[22] The swan pulling the bark in this tale is no doubt one of the animal forms of the goddess of the Otherworld.

There can be no doubt about the mythical origin of the motif of the animal psychopomp (the conductor of the soul) in the hagiographic legends of Vincent, James, and Tropez. While the simultaneous presence of a rooster and a dog at the side of Saint Tropez has been explained only in terms of vague allegories (for example, the rooster is a symbol of vigilance or of the Christian faith; the dog is a symbol of faithfulness to God), such glosses are hardly satisfying. The mystery of this animal association remains until we venture into study of the hagiographic imagination.

For instance, we might interpret the presence of the rooster near the decapitated body of Saint Tropez as an extension of the beheading motif in ancient myth. In the hagiographic legend, it is the beheaded Saint Tropez who is accompanied by a rooster, whereas in the tales of mythic origin, it is the cock himself who suffers decapitation. The "beheading" of the rooster belongs, in fact, to the Carnival rites of numerous regions.[23]

In medieval France, a Carnival custom associated with *jeudi-jeudiot* (the Thursday that precedes the Fat Days) has been reconstructed with the assistance of medieval iconographic evidence and folkloric tradition. A cockfight allowed for choosing the king of the schoolboys who would bear his temporary title during the fat days. In fact, a miniature from 1338 attests to this custom. In Portugal, there is the custom of the *piniatta* that Claude Gaignebet quite correctly puts back in the cycle of Carnival, in relation to the folklore of the cock: "On the day of Mardi Gras, a man with his eyes covered must kill a paper rooster that is filled with oranges and is called a piniatta (a word of Italian origin designating a pot)."[24] Even if it is not a living rooster, the rite echoes a sacrifice; when the custom originated, it was certainly a flesh-and-blood animal that was sacrificed on this occasion. Similarly, the game of the rooster is played in the French Alps on the day of Saint John of Summer (June 24). This involves the remnant of a kind of Carnival rite set on a date that, like a good many others, takes place at the same time as the bonfire.

This return of the sacrificed cock is explained by the recurrence of the rites and myths of Carnival on eight different dates of the year connected to the cycles of solstices or equinoxes, and by the privileged liaison between the rooster and the divine bird and the giant of the Otherworld. If this giant bearing the name of Hellequin (Hannequin,

Annequin) is very much a bird-dog (see chapter 3), we are no longer surprised at finding a bird (cock) and a dog near the beheaded corpse of Saint Tropez.

In the carnivalesque liturgy, the beheaded (or mutilated) figure is often the giant (or mannequin) of Carnival. It is a very simple step to take from this to presuming a relationship between the rooster and the key figure of the carnivalesque myth. Like the giaint, the rooster is a carnivalesque creature. The feast of Saint James the Greater (July 25) does not by chance fall close to the festival of Lughnasa, which reactualizes an aspect of the myth of Carnival: the decapitation of a Celtic god over whom the Church would superimpose the image of Saint James. There is no doubt, then, that the Manekine is confounded, mythologically speaking, with Annequin or Hennequin, meaning with the bird-dog of the Wild Hunt. As we have seen, certain Occitan versions of the story *La Manekine* specify that the child birthed by La Manekine is an ambiguous creature: dog or human child—no one knows. As for the mutilation of La Manekine (her hand is cut off), according to the text, this takes place on Candlemas (February 2) and, as with other Carnival-like rites mentioned in the text, it clearly appears as a twin of the rite of   decapitation suffered by certain animals (roosters, geese, and so on) associated with Carnival. This explains how this mutilated woman (whom some stories name Brigid and who is the reincarnation of the bird-woman) ends up traveling in the company of a dog-child on a boat abandoned to the waves on Candlemas. She has company, for the boat of Saint Vincent carries a mutilated corpse and two ravens (bird-women) and that of Saint Tropez carries a rooster, a dog, and a beheaded man.

February 3, Saint Blaise's Day

Commemorated on the day following Candlemas, Saint Blaise gathers into his person a series of mythical motifs that are essential to an understanding of the Carnival myth. The close relationship this saint maintained with animals merits emphasis because the name Blaise evokes the Breton name for wolf (*bleizh*). In fact, Blaise appears more as a humanized animal than as a man who knows animals. Once he was elected bishop of Sebasta in Armenia, he retired to a cave to exercise his apostolate. This eremitic life is the first sign of Blaise's mythic wildness, which makes him kin to the bear that figures prominently in so many tales and legends. Nevertheless, people sought him out because of his power to heal the sick in soul and body. He was also imputed to have the gift of speaking to animals in a way they could understand. This is not a unique case, for in his Topagraphia Hibernica, Giraut de Barri relates the tale of a wolf who speaks with a priest.[25] If, etymologically speaking, Blaise is a wolf, then this specific power of his does not surprise. It is, of course, necessary to see that his word is sacred. In it Christianity reveals the celestial mark: It is God who inspires the saint. Alternatively, the holy nature of this word is explained by the fact that it emanates from a seer. The pagan figure covered by the saint is most likely a kind of Wild Man, holder of all the secrets of fate.

Persecuted for his faith, Saint Blaise was led into martyrdom. Because he once cured a child who was suffocating after having swallowed a fish bone that lodged in his throat, his intercession was often sought against sore throats and animal bites. On his feast day in certain regions, it was customary to bless oil that would be applied to the throats of the ill or

Fig. 4.3. Saint Blaise

on bites. He was likewise supposed to provide protection against plague and cholers. Similarly, Saint Blaise's intercession was sought against the illnesses suffered by animals.

Here again a detour through myth helps us to understand this saint's patronage of the throat and various illnesses associated with animals. Blaise is quite like the Christian incarnation of a wolf-god. Actually, at the time of his Christianization, this archaic figure was divided into two opposing entities: Saint Blaise, whose miracles are considered holy, and the diabolical figure of the werewolf, whose disturbing powers were considered the opposite of holy. The legends of the werewolf are a folkloric reminiscence of the ancient powers of the wolf-god (or the bear-god) that originally were one with those Christianity has attributed to the Blaise of hagiographic legends.

By recalling that February 3, Saint Blaise's feast day, is the birth date of the giant Gargantua, Rabelais deliberately inserted the gargantuan myth into the Carnival tradition and religion. Simultaneously a site for speech, a place for the ingestion of food, and a place for circulation of vital breath (in German, *blasen* means "to blow"), the throat (gargantua) of Blaise echoes that of the divine wolf, the wolf-man (or the bear-man) who governs the cycles of time as well as the liturgies of Carnival. The music from wind instruments, the great feasting, the emergence of the predatory bear (or werewolf)—all are rites of time striving to establish the principles of an order providing the references humans require to define themselves.

January 17, Saint Anthony's Pig

Several days before Saint Blaise's Day is the feast of Saint Anthony (January 17). It is on this day that pigs are slaughtered, which is one of the reasons why, since the Middle Ages, the saint has always been depicted accompanied by one of these animals. It is indeed quite paradoxical to see a pig accompanying a saint of Paradise, for the Bible and the Koran have found no virtue in this animal and have saddled it with the most extreme taboos. As heir to the Hebrew scriptures, Christianity should have followed Judaism on this point, yet it did not. Views on this animal have thus become divided, with Judaism and Islam on one side and Christianity on the other.[26] The mythology of the pig is actually fascinating,[27] leading to a reevalutation of the peremptory judgments that have been made against this animal by virtue of Jewish religious taboos and forcing us to reconsider the mythic figure of the swineherd, for which Saint Anthony could well be a mythic avatar.[28]

This figure also appears in the Homeric poems in the guise of Eumeus, Ulysses' swineherd, as well as in Celtic legends in the form of Tristan, swineherd for King Mark of Cornwall. These appearances testify to a remarkable fact: The swineherd is considered not a domestic servant charged with a servile task, but, to the contrary, a royal functionary committed to privileged and valued duties. Given this, the saint accompanied by a pig is rather akin to a major initiatory figure. Although nothing in the most ancient hagiographic texts explains the presence of the pig at Saint Anthony's side, we might wonder if this animal has taken the place of the centaur and the Capricorn that Saint Jerome mentions earlier as being at Saint Anthony's side.[29] Moreover, in a Welsh medieval text, Merlin is accompanied by piglets, and these animals become the seer's confidants. This would confirm a priori the existence of a privileged bond in Celtic culture between a pig and a figure inspired by a deity (whether pagan or Christian). In making Saint Anthony a guardian of swineherds, Christianity was merely transferring the old beliefs of Indo-European paganism.

FIVE

The Transitional Period of Easter

ight periods of forty days theoretically correspond to three hundred twenty days, whereas the solar year consists of three hundred sixty-five days plus a few hours. The gap in fact comes from the interval that exists between a calendar based on the rhythms of the lunar phases (like the calendar of the so-called barbarian peoples before the Roman conquest) and a solar calendar.

The movable feast of Easter is the key to the entire medieval calendar. It introduces a dephasing in the forty-day rhythms analyzed here, but, in fact, simply confirms the principle. We know that Easter is a movable holiday that can fall between March 22 and April 25. Forty days before Easter, an early Mardi Gras can find itself much closer to Candlemas, while an Easter holiday occurring later will make Mardi Gras a month later. In the interval, Lent imposes its strictness and inflexible law of forty days (Carême—Lent—comes from the Latin *quadragesima*, which refers to "forty").

The Passage

Easter (Pâques in French) comes from the popular Latin *pascua* and the Greek *paskha* formed from the Hebrew *pesah*, meaning "passage." The Christian holiday of Easter in fact consists of a reply to the Jewish Passover. Judaism celebrates Passover in commemoration of a passage— that of the Hebrews over the Red Sea when they were pursued by the

Egyptians in the Exodus. This miraculous passage was interpreted as a salvation granted by God to his chosen people. Moses instituted Passover as an annual commemoration of the event. On this day, according to Hebrew tradition, it is necessary to sacrifice a young male lamb and eat it with unleavened bread.

While the passage over the Red Sea recalls the salvation of the Hebrew people, to Christians Christ achieved another form of passage that is also understood as a form of salvation: the passage from death to life through the Resurrection, which is commemorated on Easter. By rising from the dead, Christ gave humankind the hope of eternal life insofar as death was no longer an inevitability leading to nothingness. Theologically, the Christian "passage" thus responds to the Hebraic passage.

The Jews celebrate Passover on the fourteenth day of the month of Nizan (corresponding to March). At the Council of Nicaea in 325 C.E., the Christians, somewhat appropriating the Jews' custom, decided to celebrate Easter on the first Sunday following the full moon of the spring equinox, which thus made it a movable feast that even today falls on a different date every year.

A festival of springtime and the equinox and a lunar festival, Easter is connected to a seasonal myth that contains several superimposed meanings. It is not by chance that the resurrection of Christ is celebrated during the return of spring. In this moment of renewal there is a kind of cosmic necessity. The resurrection of nature finds its sacred justification in the rising of Christ. Furthermore, in mythology it is not at all rare to see seasonal rites continue from one civilization to the next. Therefore, through Easter we can hear various echoes of the pagan myths that preceded the entry of the gospels and Christianity into the West.

Eating

Since the earliest years of the Church, the date of Easter has constituted a major concern for the organizers of the liturgical calendar. Quite obviously, the clergy quickly grasped the strategic value of this festival in the process of the Christianization of pagan religions. The later institution of Lent as a preparatory period for Easter, with the prohibition on eating meat, was a deliberate response to the desire to remove the excesses of the Carnival-like festivities that were viewed as impious.

In fact, sacrificial libations, revelry, and ritual meals of Christmas, Easter, Saint John's Day, and Saint Michael's Day appear fundamentally connected to the pre-Christian cycle of pagan festivals. Among the Scandinavians, the carnivalesque feasting of the Jol feast (Christmas) responded to the same need to religiously consume the sacred animal of the clan (boar and pork for the Germans, beef and pork for the Celts), as if this rite permitted the accomplishment and renewal of the sacred time that gave meaning to the entire society. Animal sacrifices perhaps replaced human sacrifices that held a similar function: in the words of Georges Dumézil, to realize on earth a sort of "feast of immortality."[1]

Though it wanted to eliminate libations and ritual feasts, the Church tolerated them by granting them a precarious status precisely within a rite. It thus inserted them for a strictly circumscribed period of time and in so doing constructed the religious opposition of two periods of time (that of Carnival and that of Lent) in order to better explain the Pascal message, for around the time of Easter there is a wide scope of Christian interpretation of the pagan myths appropriated by Christianity. It was necessary for the Church to maintain a portion of the pagan practices to allow for a better understanding of the very meaning of Christianity.

The rites of the table were at the heart of this mechanism. In fact, it is truly the wager of food that best defines the Pascal period. For the Jewish Passover, the ritual consumption of lamb and unleavened bread formed the principal rite of the holiday. For Christianity, it was the installation of the Eucharist by Christ on the night before his Passion that served as the Christian answer to the Hebrew rite of the Pascal lamb.

The institution of the Eucharist, the major mystery of Christianity, is recalled during every celebration of the Mass. During the last supper he shared with his disciples, Christ took bread, blessed it, broke it, and gave it to his followers, saying: "Take this and eat, for this is my body." Then, taking a chalice, he blessed the wine and gave it to his disciples, saying: "This is the chalice of my blood." The Christian Communion instituted around Easter therefore corresponds to the ritual consumption of the body and the blood of God—in other words, a theophagy (from *theos,* meaning "God," and *phagein,* meaning "eat"). Yet this theophagy also presents itself as anthropophagy, because God has been made human by his Incarnation. When taking Communion at Mass, the Christian is therefore eating the flesh both of a man and of God.

It is therefore not possible to disassociate the Eucharist meal from a cannibal ritual, if we understand *cannibalism* to imply the simultaneously real and symbolic consumption of sacred flesh. Mythology offers us numerous examples of such practices, from the cult of Dionysus, which served as a pretext for eating human flesh, to that of Thyestes' feast, in which he ate his own children. Yet with respect to this subject it is the figure of Cronos who is the most suggestive. After marrying his own sister and making himself master of the world, Cronos learns that he will be dethroned by one of his own children. This leads to his custom of eating them at birth. The wordplay (in ancient Greek) between Cronos and *chronos* (time) immediately encourages a temporal interpretation of the myth. The devouring activity of the ogre-god Cronos offers an image of the destructive power of time (chronos). In other words, all consumption of human flesh signifies the wearing away, even the death, of the world. By reversing the terms of the relationship, Christianity claims, on the contrary, to be rejuvenating humanity, for by eating the Christ-God during Communion, Christians take the food of immortality.

A major work of medieval literature is a gloss of this myth. In the twelfth century, the symbolism of the Grail was founded on the ambiguity of a meal that was both profane and sacred. Constructed on an ancient theophagic rite of Celtic origin, the tale of the Grail opposes a sumptuous profane feast to the sacred meal that consists of a single host placed in the Grail.[2] In Chrétien de Troyes's *Story of the Grail,* the destiny of Perceval, the first literary figure to encounter the Grail, is fulfilled during the meditation of the Pascal mystery, from Good Friday to Easter Sunday, for these three days contain the essential spiritual message of medieval Christianity.

During the Middle Ages, sorcerers rites played a large role in cannibal practices. In the eleventh century, traces of this can be found with Burchard of Worms, who condemns the "belief of numerous women in Satan's entourage" and the deed "of killing with invisible weapons Christians who have been baptized and redeemed by the blood of Christ, to eat their flesh after having it cooked, and to replace their heart with straw or a piece of wood or some other object." Then, "after having eaten [these] victims, to resurrect them and grant them an additional span of life."[3] Far from appearing as displays of the specific manifestations of a Satanic antireligion, these rites of sorcery smack more of a systematization of practices that preceded Christianity—practices the Church had rejected. Holy or Good Friday, a traditional Sabbath date during the Middle Ages, constituted a direct reply to the dubious practices of paganism, for, according to the Church, Christ offered himself as an eternal victim to put an end to all the human and animal sacrifices of pre-Christian religions. To respect Lent and take Communion at Easter is to deny the excesses of Carnival and the instinct toward a morbid desire that motivates the witch or sorcerer.

A large devouring figure, that of the giant-ogre, haunts Carnival and also haunts diabolic iconography through the image of the gaping jaws of hell. The figure of the devil is formed from all the imaginary ogres of the Middle Ages, which themselves were mere descendants from ancient pre-Christian myths. The devil is, by definition, the infernal cannibal.

When we closely examine them, the many stories of werewolves constitute many decomposed forms of ancient initiation rites that were connected to the ancient belief in the Double.[4] Marie de France relates the story of a wolf-man in one of her lays. In this she shows evidence of a belief that could easily explain the Christian prohibition on eating meat on Fridays. In *Bisclavret,* she notes that the cursed man becomes a wolf three days during the week. What are these three days? Could they be the weekend, including Friday and the Sabbath? These are the days around which gravitate several taboos belonging to that dangerous period of time during which men can be transformed into wolves. This is precisely the moment when the Sabbaths are held, for on these dangerous days were concentrated all threats. It became necessary to arm Christians against the dangers such threats represented by forbidding them, for example, to eat meat on Fridays. Those who ignored this prohibition revealed themselves as true witches and sorcerers devoted to ogrelike practices. The Christian explanation, according to which the fast of Friday was implemented to commemorate the death of Christ, appears to be merely a posteriori reasoning. What is involved here is actually the consumption of a flesh originally imagined as a sacred food and one that returns man to a state of divine animality. Before becoming the embodiment of the devil, the werewolf is in reality the animal form of a deity; he is the wolf-god or the wolf-man, a sacred being in a state of temporary metamorphosis and migration that Christianity is incapable of tolerating.

The Egg

Like the other seven major dates of the year, Easter can be understood as a date marking an intense circulation between the Otherworld and the human world. The model for these relations can be found in numerous Celtic tales, but the Christic passage from death into life reproduces this symbolic journey in terms of Christianity. In folklore, the Pascal period is marked first and foremost by the apparition of beings from the Otherworld who take on animal shapes. The Easter Bunny, for example, is a springtime reincarnation of the Wild and belongs among the host of magical animals that haunted the medieval imagination.

While those in the Middle Ages did not recognize the rabbit that distributed gifts and sweets, they did know other, equally marvelous figures. The white doe or white stag of the Arthurian tales haunts the transitions that separate the forty-day periods of the year. In Chrétien de Troyes's romance *Erec and Enide,* the hunt of the white stag takes place on Easter Monday, as if there was a need to recall the connection between this animal and the moon of the equinox. In fact, the lunar body governs the appearance of fairy animals and provides the rhythm of their annual reappearance, while these soul-guiding animals serve as mediators between the human world and the Otherworld.

In modern folklore, traditional Easter eggs are supposedly carried to children by the bells on their way back from Rome or by the Easter Bunny himself. In Germanic regions, however, this role of the enchanted rabbit is played by entirely different animals: In Westphalia it is a fox, in Thuringia a stork, in the Tyrol a white hen, in Switzerland a cuckoo, and in Saxony a rooster. It seems that most often farmyard animals accompany these ritual eggs. Yet it is obvious that Easter eggs are invested with a mythical value that has nothing to do with their usual role as food. In fact, their mythic character gives greater value to their nonfood meaning. As for the Easter Bunny, its mythic role is much older than Christian civilization, for it can be found in ancient Buddhist and Chinese mythology.[5] According to these myths, a rabbit lives on the moon, where he prepares the food of immortality. Easter eggs seem analogous to this food, although it is obviously not possible to establish a direct link between them and the food of the ancient Chinese deities.

In folklore, however, Easter eggs, especially those laid on Good Friday, were regarded as being capable of bestowing health on both men and beasts. They could be stored for a long time, afforded protection against lightning, and could be used to both uncover and disarm witches. It was said that ingesting a soup with a base of nine different vegetables and herbs could also accomplish this. Today, the Easter egg still offers protection as a good-luck charm. In certain regions of Alsace, vintage eggs are handed down through generations. Further, it is believed that the yolk of an Easter egg preserved for one hundred years will transform into a precious stone and ensure the fortune of its owner.

The druids of an earlier era also believed in the magical power of the egg. The Gallic myth of the *vouivre* (winged serpent), recorded by the Latin writer Pliny, sums up these characteristics. Marcel Aymé illustrated this belief in an amusing way in one of his novels in which he explicitly refers to this ancient Gallic tradition. It is said that this mythical animal secreted a kind of egg that could be turned into a talisman. The figure of the vouivre, a conglomeration of all the magical creatures of the Otherworld, could certainly represent a belief in the periodic regeneration of time within a season, a kind of human molting or rebirth.

The Instruments of Darkness

The Easter festival is the symbolic interpretation of a passage from one season to the next, the passage from the death of winter to the life of springtime. Easter can be compared to certain pagan festivals that coincide with the spring equinox. These festivals have allowed rituals to survive that have been so seamlessly integrated into the Christian commemorations that their pagan origin can no longer be discerned.

In certain regions there still exists the practice of making the rounds with rattles on the Friday and Saturday before Easter. During the temporary absence of the bells that have left for Rome, the children shake their rattles and thus keep the villagers informed of the schedule of church services. Lepers likewise rattled during the Middle Ages to warn people of their presence. In Béroul's twelfth-century romance *Tristan,* rattles were called *tartarie,* perhaps harkening to Tartary, which Christians viewed as identical to the domain of the devil. One of the prayers said for a funeral Mass includes these words: "Lord Jesus, king of glory, deliver the souls of all the deceased faithful from the tortures of hell and the bottomless lake (*de profundo lacu*). Deliver them from the lion's jaw, that they may not be swallowed by Tartary (*ne absorbeat eas Tartarus*)." The Tartary* of ancient Greece survived in Christianity to designate the infernal river, which the soul would have to cross once it left its dead body.

Around the eighth century, it became customary to stop using bells during the three days before Easter, though this custom was not codified in the liturgical manuals until the ninth century. From the Thursday to Saturday before Easter, all metal bells were banished and replaced by wooden instruments. Claude Lévi-Strauss has mentioned a comparable custom in ancient China that took place at the same time of the year.[6] In the twelfth century, the custom of using these "instruments of darkness" was observed throughout the West. Although this pagan custom made its way into Christianity quite early on, in order to grasp its meaning, it is necessary to turn once more to medieval folklore.

---

*[Tartary also refers to the Asian region east of the Urals, although in the Middle Ages it served as a blanket term for any place that was in neither Europe nor Africa. —*Trans.*]

The ritual production of a specific noise is characteristic of the Pascal period. The word in old French used to describe this noisy commotion is *rabast,* and folklore generally attributes the cause of rabast to goblins or small demons. Some have even tried to establish a lingusitic connection between this term and the term Sabbath. In fact, the din caused by rattles was intended to drown out the noise made by demons, the better to exorcise them. Bells are the instruments normally used for the exorcism of demons, for it is said that their sound sends fleeing the evil spirits that infest the air. When the bells disappeared and could not be used, it became necessary to find substitute instruments that could perform the same apotropaic function. In some of Brueghel's engravings, there are figures chasing devils with hammer blows, but it is in the ritual hullabaloo that we can find the practice of creating noise associated with a myth and a rite that justifies its existence.

Purgatory and March 17, Saint Patrick's Day

In the heart of the equinoctial period, the great Celtic saint of transition, Saint Patrick, the national hero of Ireland, is celebrated on March 17. We can find mention of his feast day in the ancient martyrologies of Bede, Florus, Adon, Raban Maur, and Usuard. We should also note that Patrick is celebrated not only in Ireland, but in Scotland, France, and Spain as well.

There exist several different versions of the life of the saint. The oldest of these date from the second half of the seventh century and are emblematic of a vast movement of Christianization that was then affecting Celtic paganism. The *Life of Saint Patrick* is an odd blend of chronicle, edifying story, and marvelous legend. It is also and perhaps primarily a prodigious assemblage of Celtic mythic motifs and biblical themes.[7] What can be perceived therein are the methods of Christianization that touched the very depths of Celtic beliefs attached to Irish soil.

Saint Patrick is clearly associated with what is known as the hole of Purgatory—that is, the belief according to which it is possible to enter into and travel in the Otherworld, which became Christianized as the

Purgatory. The hole on the Isle of Derg through which, it is said, Purgatory can be reached is not an imaginary site. This abyss was reworked into a vaulted construction, probably during prehistoric times, and in the very remote past served as a chamber of visions. Perhaps it was the home for certain rites and mysteries similar to those practiced in the cave of Trophonius[8] and transported to Ireland at the beginning of the Christian era. Certainly the place calls to mind the esoteric rites specific to old shamanic customs that had been reintroduced into the Celtic religion. During the Middle Ages, at the time of the reign of Henry II Plantagenet (1154–89), monks built a monastery on the Isle of Regis and organized a kind of pilgrimage descent into the hole of Saint Patrick, placing under the saint's authority the rites of voyaging to the Otherworld, which had become Purgatory.[9]

Indeed, Purgatory has all the appearances of being a Christian reformulation of the Celtic Otherworld, which is increasingly confused with the world of the dead, though it was originally the dwelling of gods and magical beings. As for Saint Patrick, his commemoration during the Pascal period and his association with a mythical Otherworld brings to mind an obvious comparison to Christ, who went down into hell after his death to free the souls of the just. This infernal voyage is suggestive of many others in countless mythologies that tell of a crossing to death (*catabasis*) followed almost immediately by a return to the human world.[10] The god or demigod psychopomps that accomplish fairly perilous journeys often act in obedience to cosmic injunctions. Thus their voyage to the Beyond is most often inscribed inside a sacred time and space that the calendrical rites periodically maintain and remember.

April 14, the Day of Saint Benezet, Bridge Builder and Boatman

Saint Benezet,* another saint involved with "crossing over," is commemorated during the Pascal period. Although his legend has remained

---

*[Saint Benezet is also known as Saint Benedict the Bridge Builder or Little Saint Benedict. —*Trans.*]

removed from the great hagiographies, it nevertheless holds many interesting aspects that shed light on the Pascal myth of passage in its pre-Christian form.

We know of the life of Saint Benezet thanks to a thirteenth-century old Provençal text[11] accompanied by acts written in Latin. Of course, it is all too easy to underscore the unlikelihood of a legend or tradition that some have sought to pass off as a historical truth. Yet at times it is precisely such legends that are capable of revealing the pagan mind-set that was reworked by Christian hagiography. As we have seen, rigorous historical study has yet to come to grips with such documents, which might well lead to a simple annihilation of a particular saint's tradition, for in many cases these legends are the sole objective reference in a subject.

Saint Benezet is celebrated on April 14, a springtime date that reveals the original pagan aspects of Easter (which might fall as late as April 25). Benezet, who built the bridge of Avignon, has remained, in the legendary tradition, a boatman and a pontiff (in Latin *pontifex* means "bridge builder"). This bridge enabled people to cross a particularly dreaded river in a city, Avignon, that later became (is this mere chance?) the seat of the papacy and its sovereign pontiffs from 1309 to 1377. Given that Easter is above all the feast of the passage of Christ from life to death, then death to life, Saint Benezet serves in part to explain the great myth of this equinoctial season occurring during the Pascal period: Like Christ, who went down into hell to free the souls of the just and give them passage to eternal life, Benezet helps the souls of men pass from one bank of the river of time to the other. We can recall the figure of Charon, the ferryman of souls, who also haunts the life of Benezet, who had to appeal to a ferryman in order to fulfill his mission as a bridge builder. According to the *Life of Benezet*:

On the day when an eclipse of the sun occurred, a child named Benezet was guarding his mother's flock of sheep in the pasture when a voice from the sky suddenly commanded him: "I want you to leave your mother's sheep to build me a bridge over the Rhone." In response to the child's reservations, the voice promised to watch over the sheep and to provide him with a companion who would lead him to the Rhone. Benezet then met an angel who had taken on the appearance of a pilgrim carrying a staff and a beggar's haversack. This individual led him to Avignon, showed him a Jewish boatman who could take him across the river in return for a small donation, and advised him to present himself before the bishop.

When Benezet came before the prelate, he revealed to the bishop the purpose of his mission. He was made the object of mockery and scorn, but the city's provost told him: "What the heck! You who are the least of men and who own nothing, you boast you can make a bridge where neither God nor Saint Peter nor Saint Paul nor Charlemagne himself nor anyone else could! All right, because a bridge is made from stones and lime, I will give you a stone I have in my palace. If you can carry it, then I do believe you will be able to build the bridge."

Benezet took the stone that thirty men could not have lifted and carried it with as much ease as if it were a simple pebble. This was how he inspired the admiration and conversion of the people of Avignon. He then went on to heal many who were sick because God performed miracles thanks to him.

The Royal Shepherd

The significance of Benezet's humble occupation as shepherd can be better understood in the light of the legendary biographies of various illustrious figures. We can explore some revealing comparisons between the modest Provençal shepherd and some major historical or mythical figures to discover that though there is a stunning contrast between Benezet's social origins and the mission he is called upon to fulfill, this apparent contradiction can be easily explained by mythology.

In an article entitled "The Royal Legend of Ancient Iran," G. Widengren has shown that there is a clearly defined type of Iranian legend and, even more broadly, an Indo-European legend that recounts the ascension of a figure from obscurity to royalty.[12] According to myth, shepherds raise this future king during his youth. The legends of Cyrus, Mithradate Eupator, Romulus, and Antaxerxes conform to this model. Likewise Perceval in the Arthurian cycle, who is raised in the forest, far from courts and knights, a veritable simpleton at the beginning of his adventures, belongs to this group of future kings with rustic origins, even if he somewhat disappoints us by failing the test at the Grail Castle. Through this episode, he is confronted with a test of sovereignty that might have earned him royal consecration.

Lithobolia, or the Gargantuan Exploit

According to the story, Benezet builds the bridge of Avignon on his own by first moving a gigantic stone located in the palace of the city's provost.* Of course, he performs this task with disconcerting ease through his Herculean strength.

The saint's vigor here cannot help but bring to mind that of a very well-known figure in French folklore: Jean de l'Ours (John of the Bear). This fairy-tale hero obtains his extraordinary strength from a unique birth: He is the son of a bear and a young woman the bear kidnapped and carried off to a cavern. According to his story, upon coming into his strength, Jean de l'Ours picks up and removes the stone that has blocked the cave in which he and his mother have been imprisoned since his birth. As the story progresses, his first apprenticeship with a peasant gives him the opportunity to deploy his prodigious strength.

This uncommon muscular prowess is also reminiscent of the Gargantuan exploits[13] similar to the great Herculean feats in the Indo-European world. It is analogous also to the strength of Lancelot, who, in a famous episode from Chrétien de Troyes's *Knight of the Cart,* picks up the tombstone in the cemetery in which he is to be buried after his death. We can note that in all these examples, the strength of the hero is displayed as he deals with moving a particularly heavy stone. We might conclude that these stones are in some way related to

---

*[In the Languedoc, a provost is a *viguier.* —*Trans.*]

the origin of megaliths. The similarities between the Herculean gesture of Lancelot and that of Benezet undoubtedly suggest the presence of a common mythic archetype behind both figures. Lancelot is summoned to fulfill a superhuman destiny, the destiny of a sovereign. His liaison with Queen Guinevere, figure of female sovereignty, theoretically lifts him to the rank of king, which poses real problems with Arthur, the queen's legitimate husband.

In the personalities of Gargantua, Lancelot, and Benezet there can be seen the motif of *lithobolia,* the myths and legends concerning foundation. As F. Delpech explains,[14] "in the legendary tales about the construction of bridges, *lithobolia* (or the more or less supernatural moving of the stones by a saint or demon builder) provides an echo of more clearly cosmogonic traditions on the formation of the relief of a particular landscape by a supernatural being: giant, Virgin, or fairy." The various characters of this thematic lithobolia reflect a unique being whose mythic nature is obvious. When this figure cannot be canonized like Benezet, Christianity gives it diabolical features.

The Bridge of the Devil

The stone-carrying devil (*lou diable porto peiro*) is an old Provençal tradition with which Frédéric Mistral was well acquainted. The *félibrige** poet used it for the epigraph of his poem *Nerto,* which recalls the mission of this mythical creature in various desperate building situations, in particular the construction of bridges.

In Celtic legends, Arthurian tales, and related folklore, the bridge is a major mythical site. We need only recall Chrétien de Troyes's fairylike and mysterious Bridge of the Sword or Bridge of Glass in the Grail story. We can also turn to the traditions and legends of European folklore: In all Celtic lands and throughout the Indo-European world—truly a Euro-Asiatic basis—there are legends related to the bridge of the devil.

---

*[The Félibrige was a group formed by Frédéric Mistral and six fellow poets who sought to promote the arts and language of their native Provence. —*Trans.*]

According to these, the cunning one built bridges in the hope of snaring souls as payment, but at the last minute he is thwarted by a saint or is caught short by the break of day. The Segovia aqueduct, the bridge of Martorell, and the Toledo legend of the bridge of San Martin all respond to this model.[15]

By all evidence, the devil is a figure who conveniently serves to cover another, traditional figure whose mythical stature we can easily discern.[16] The legends of the devil's bridges mask the presence of a pagan deity who has been given the features of Satan. This hero bridge builder was originally a giant possessing magical powers, and, in fact, an episode from *The Prose Tristan* seems to provide us with his name: To subject to a test the knights errant that were crossing his lands, a lord named Argan constructed a bridge where he would meet in combat every knight desiring to cross it.[17] Isn't this bridge of Argan reminiscent of a bridge originally constructed by the fairy giant Gargantua? It even seems that the lord Argan's name is contained in the name of the giant: *Gargan*tua. In fact, there exists twelfth-century literature featuring a mythical giant that allows us to confirm a form of this name before Rabelais wrote of Gargantua.

In his valuable dictionary, the Reverend Father Cahier[18] has related a typical legend[19] concerning Saint Cado on the bridge of the devil.

It is told in Armorica that after leaving Great Britain, Saint Cado founded a monastery on a small island between Port Louis and Auray, at the mouth of the Estell. The local people gladly went there and the saint, wishing to facilitate their passage, joined his island to the mainland with a stone bridge that he had to start to build again after a first unsuccessful attempt. But his second attempt was successful and the work appeared wonderful to the local folk, and this gave rise to those stories that are told repeatedly in various regions about what are called the bridges of the devil. It was therefore said that the demon had demolished the first construction and that Saint Cado, finding the devil busy at his wicked task, asked the evil one what he would want if he would build the bridge. The cunning one promised to perform the task on condition that he be allowed to seize the first soul that crossed the bridge. Once the job was completed, the saint came before the demon and released from his sleeve a large cat. Deceived in this way, Satan no longer appeared in the area.

In an identical scenario, the devil offers his assistance in the construction of the famous Brunehaut Causeway in the north of France.[20] Likewise, in *The Rhine* Victor Hugo recalls an identical tradition concerning the cathedral of Strasbourg: After having taken part in the construction of the building, the devil is thwarted by swallowing a wolf in the place of a soul.

Popular memory has unknowingly preserved another mythological tradition concerning the bridge of Avignon built by the fairy-giant substitute, Saint Benezet. The song* is so famous today that no one dreams anymore of questioning its content. According to its words, people dance in a circle on Avignon Bridge. In the Middle Ages, this circle dance was called a carol. *The Romance of the Rose* elevated it to the status of art and the miniaturists did not fail to depict it. In 1940 Margit Sahlin[21] devoted a wide-ranging study to the circle dance, which, despite several philologically uncertain hypotheses, remains very pertinent scholarship. If we are to believe medieval literature, this circle dance often appeared in connection with certain sites and ritual dates such as the solstices and, more generally, the changing of the seasons, which confirms its mythical nature.

The oldest mention of the carol in a text dates from the twelfth century,[22] but the dance is certainly much, much older. We can certainly envision the ritual origins of this circle dance practiced at specific times of the year at certain stone-covered sites. The circle dance on the bridge of Avignon[23] is thus not accidentally associated with a bridge whose legendary construction required the intervention of a particularly robust young man who was capable of moving a megalith. Indeed, we can find

---

*[The song refers to "Sur le Pont d'Avignon." —*Trans.*]

the association of the magical rite of the circle dance with megaliths in the legend of Merlin: After the battle against the Saxons, Uther had the memorial of Salisbury erected with Merlin's aid. These stones, moved from Ireland through Merlin's druidic magic, carried the name *querole as jaianz,* "carol of the giants,"* according to a manuscript conserved by the municipal library of Tours.

The case of Benezet is simply a variation on the motif that remains functionally connected to the same context: People dance in a circle on the bridge, whereas the Irish stones dance themselves (through Merlin's magic). This motif of the dancing stones is well known in French folklore. Paul Sébillot and Pierre Saintyves have recorded legends of stones that dance, drink, and even bathe.[24] The movement of these stones is connected to certain times of the year (solstices and equinoxes), and because they move, they allow entrance to the Otherworld, which they otherwise guard and block.

Avignon, the Bridge and the City of the Pontiffs

In Celtic mythology the bridge builder who establishes a junction between the banks of a river is always an exceptional being. In fact, the Celtic hero Bran made his very body a bridge to enable his men to cross a river, calling out as he did so, "Let he who is chief be a bridge!"

The bridge possesses eschatological symbolism in shamanic tradition. It took on spiritual and political significance in both the Roman world and the Middle Ages. Roman emperors originally carried the title of sovereign pontiff. Its medieval transfer to the Church's leaders can probably be explained by the symbolic meaning granted to both the bridge and the pontificate. For Romans, the pontiff was a minister of the cult responsible for the management of the calendar and religious holidays. He therefore asserted himself as a kind of master of time, which is the definitive role of Benezet, who, by his work as a pontiff bridge builder, opened the road to the Beyond to the wandering souls in search of eternity.

---

*[This might also be translated as "dance of the giants." —*Trans.*]

The life of Saint Benezet constitutes the Christianized episode of a myth in which a fairy giant (such as the Gargantua of folk legends), or even a simple fairy (such as Melusine), transported megaliths for the building and founding of sacred sites. This motif is confirmed by the storehouse of French legends. Reincarnated in Benezet is the figure of a pontiff ferryman, a veritable master of time and passage, capable of guiding humans over the secret paths of the Otherworld during the middle of the Pascal period. Easter was thus a Christianized version of a double tradition: It constituted a Christian reply to the Jewish Passover and gave a Christian dimension to the great Celtic myths of passage to the Otherworld. The labor of Benezet can be combined with that of Martin, Blaise, and Christopher, who, during the great rifts of time, commemorate the same mystery of passage.

SIX

May 1, Beltane

I n ancient Rome, the month of May, consecrated to the ancestors (*majores*), witnessed the incursion of ghosts among the living. The key date of May 1 permits another opportunity for the fairy world to break through to the human world. During antiquity and the entire Middle Ages, marriage was avoided at all costs during the month of May because of the great risk of taking as a spouse a revenant or an enchanted woman from the Otherworld. Because of these grim associations, May became known as the month of dragons.[1]

Coinciding with the ancient Celtic festival of Beltane,[2] the festival of May 1 recalls the great mythical themes that accompany the alternation of the seasons.

The May Queen

The rites and myths of May revolve around plants and flowers. The noble ladies and handsome knights depicted in the miniature *Très Riches Heures* of the Duke de Berry are wearing hats fashioned from flowers and leaves. Various chronicles recount the joyous festivities of spring. A herald of arms of the dukes of Burgundy, Lefèvre de Saint-Rémy, who wrote the chronicle for the years 1408–36,[3] reported that in 1414:

Milord Hector, bastard of Bourbon, instructed the peoples of Compiègne that on the first day of May he would come *gather the may*

113

for them, which thing he did, riding horseback in the company of two hundred of the most valiant men of arms escorted by footmen. All together, each having a May hat over his holiday harness, would go to the gate of Compiègne, bringing with them a large Maypole *to gather the may* for the folk of said city.

The custom, consisting of cutting and planting a maypole, has endured over the centuries and still survives in several remote areas of Europe.

Quite obviously, in urban civilization people do not plant a great many maypoles and very little remains of this custom except for the picking of lilies of the valley.* Yet during the thirteenth century, romances such as *The Romance of the Rose* and *William of Dôle* by Jean Renart recall the existence of the custom of gathering the may on May Day (May 1). It was customary to go into the forests to cull leafy branches or uproot young trees in order to replant them in front of the homes of those to be honored. The rite of May Day is arranged exactly opposite the rite of Christmas and is its springtime counterpart. Of course, this rite reflects a myth: Behind the profusion of foliage and green trees is hidden one that is sometimes called the spirit of the plants—one who is none other than the Wild Man.

The Wild Man of Candlemas reappears on May 1 in the guise of the Green Man, a creature clad entirely in leaves and branches. Thus the return of spring heralds the reappearance of the man or woman who embodies the secret and untamed forces of nature. This springtime belief in the Wild Man is also permeated with eroticism, according to the bishop of Worms, who speaks of "women called sylphs inhabiting the fields, who have a physical body. These sylphs, when the desire moves them, reveal themselves to their lovers and take their pleasure with them; when it is their desire, they hide themselves and disappear."[4]

The festivals of May provide an opportunity to celebrate the one who embodies the renewal of spring and the return of nature. French

---

*[On May Day in France it is still customary for people to give to one another stems of lily of the valley as a present and good-luck charm. —*Trans.*]

lyric poetry, taking on such springtime themes, has sometimes been described as a natural emanation of the May festivals. Although this theory appears somewhat exaggerated today, it does emphasize the trace of folklore present in this poetic tradition.

There are other lyric verses dedicated to this time. An anonymous dance song celebrates the queen of April (or the May Queen), a key figure of this period:

> *At the coming of clear weather*
> *To revive the gaiety, hola*
> *And for the jealous one scorned, hola*
> *The queen wishes to show*
> *How amorous she is*
> *Away from here, away from here, jealous one.*
> *Leave us be, leave us be*
> *Dancing together, together.*
> *She has inspired all to shout, hola*
> *That to the very edge of the sea, hola*
> *There are no maids or young men, hola*
> *Who will not come dance*
> *In the joyful dance.*
> *Away from here . . .*
> *The king comes from his side, hola.*
> *To disperse the dance, hola.*
> *For he is worried, hola.*
> *That one might seek to steal from him*
> *The April Queen.*
> *Away from here . . .*
> *But vain the effort of he who would try, hola*
> *For she has no thought to spare for an old man, hola.*
> *But of a fickle young man, hola.*
> *Who knows well how to cajole*
> *The delicious lady.*
> *Away from here . . .*[5]

In this song, the April queen is the object of a dispute between an older jealous man and a very handsome young man who will obtain from her all the favors for which he asks. In its simplicity, this springtime trio is reminiscent of the Greek myth of Persephone. Hades, the god of the Underworld, falls in love with the young Persephone, who is picking flowers in the company of nymphs. Hades abducts the young girl and carries her off to Hades. Sought by her mother, Demeter, Persephone is partially restored to the bosom of her family through Zeus's intervention, but she must henceforth share her life between the kingdom of the Underworld and that of Light.

This Greek myth is probably intended as an explanation for the changing of the seasons: the symbolic succession of summer and winter, the clear season and the overcast season. A Celtic version of the same myth served as the mythological source for the legend of Tristan and Yseult: According to the proposal offered by Arthur in the *Ystorya Trystan* (a fifteenth-century Welsh text), Yseult, avatar of the great goddess, is to be shared by the two men who claim her. For six months she must live with Mark, her winter husband, and during the other six months with her summer lover, Tristan.

The legendary life of Saint Gengout (or Gangulf), whose feast day is celebrated on May 11, reinscribes the mythical drama of the unfaithful wife within a small hagiographic novel. Before becoming a saint, Gangulf was an unlucky knight who suspected his wife of infidelity. The story tells us that one day, after his return from war, he subjects her to an intense interrogation, during which his wife pretends to be indignant and outraged. Gangulf then takes her to a spring and asks her to dip her hand in it to prove her chastity, according to the custom of the ordeal. The young woman plunges her hand into the spring but must pull it out quickly because the water begins to boil. Furthermore, her hand has become completely black and is decomposed like the stump of a leper. Gangulf then seals his wife inside the hide of a cow and throws her into a river on which she drifts for eternity. Today, the Saint Gangulf pilgrimage to Lautenbach (near Guebwiller, in the Upper Rhine) is greatly renowned. It is even said that the spring to be found there can heal illnesses of the eyes and skin. As for Saint Gangulf himself, he became the patron saint for deceived husbands and is honored in Alsace, Lorraine, Beauvaisis, and Champagne.

We can readily find a medieval text that suggests the mythological origin of this tradition and connects it to an authentic Celtic precursor. Among the mythological Irish texts transcribed during the Middle Ages (which had been passed on orally for several centuries in Ireland before being written) is a story entitled *The Courtship of Etaine*.[6] Boann, the wife of the god Nechtan, deceives her husband with the Dagda (good god) and, unbeknownst to Nechtan, gives birth to Oengus. Nechtan owns a spring with marvelous powers, and Boann, bathing in this spring, suffers three different assaults from its water: First, the spring takes away her thigh, then one of her eyes, and finally a hand. She is then pursued by this water, which eventually swallows her, after which she is transformed into a sacred river.*

Even if this mythological Irish text does not form the direct source of the legend of Saint Gangulf, it is evident that a similar tradition, probably part of oral tradition, existed on the very site where Gangulf is worshipped. The Irish and Gallic traditions refer to a common source: The parallel presence of the Irish text makes it possible to corroborate the existence of specifically Gallic traditions from which medieval Christian hagiography constructed its legendary references.

The Virgin and the Fairy

The May queen was Christianized during the Middle Ages in the figure of the Virgin Mary. The month of May therefore became the month of Mary, as if to disqualify the ancient mother goddess in the interest of Christianity.

In the thirteenth century, in his *Imperial Recreations* (Otia imperialia), Gervase of Tilbury[7] alludes to beliefs that wild beings haunt certain regions: "Many men have declared, based on their own experience or

---

*[This river is traditionally considered to be the Boyne. —*Trans.*]

that of trustworthy witnesses, that they have see Sylvan creatures and Pans, also called *incubi* or, by the Gauls, *dusii*." He goes on to say that these aerial demons could couple with humans. It seems that the word *dusii* was retained in reference to these creatures. Interestingly, in Alsace the Virgin is honored at a place that has been called Dusenbach—recalling Gervase's dusii—since the thirteenth century. Dusenbach might be translated as the River (*Bach* in German) of the Incubi or, to use another word, fairies.

A legend associated with this Marial cult in Alsace has a pseudo-historical explanation that does not succeed in obliterating the pagan myth beneath: Having rebelled against Emperor Adolph of Nassau, Anselm of Colmar was imprisoned in Swabia. There he promised to build a chapel to the Virgin if she could gain him his freedom. He was subsequently released on Purification Day (February 2), but forgot his debt of gratitude to the Virgin. Instead, he devoted himself to a life of pleasure and amusements. One day, he was hunting a stag that threw itself into a gulf. Unable to restrain his horse, both Anselm and his mount likewise tumbled into the abyss. Yet the nobleman suffered no harm from his fall. Anselm attributed his salvation to the Virgin and recalled the vow he had made. To this day the site is known as Saut du Cerf (Deer's Leap). A profane version of the same episode figures in the twelfth-century romance of Tristan, who is said to have left the imprint of his feet in a rock that henceforth bore the name Saut Tristan (Tristan's Leap).[8]

The formal pilgrimages that take place in honor of the Virgin during the month of May are beyond count. The places where the Virgin is worshipped are quite often found in the proximity of springs, trees, or stones haunted by the ancient presence of fairies or deities of the Otherworld. In Brittany, the megalithic site of Lockmariaker was consecrated to the Virgin Mary as if to exorcise the presence of the old Celtic deities. Even in the fifteenth century, belief in fairies had not been totally eliminated from certain regions. During Joan of Arc's trial, it was recorded that on the eve of Ascension (which always falls in May) the priest of Domrémy had gone to sing the gospel near the "tree of the fairies" or the "tree of the Ladies," *Ladies* being the common designation for fairies in folklore, as we can see here and there by the Ladies' Way,* for example. The ladies gradually gave way to Our Lady, who, if we are to believe the literary tradition of the *Miracles of Our Lady,* performed marvels that were even more extraordinary than those performed by her fairy predecessors.

Thus, in the city of Arras, Our Lady cured people of the plague known as *mal des ardents* using the Holy Candle, a miraculous taper that she offered to two *trouvères*.† The legend associated with the pilgrimage and worship of Our Lady of the Ardents goes thus: During the night of May 24 or 25, two trouvères of Arras, though far away from each other, had the same vision. A woman dressed in white appeared to them and said:

> Arise, my son, and find Bishop Lambert, who rules the church of Arras. One hundred forty four patients are enduring mortal suffering there. You will command him to keep vigil in the church on the night of Saturday into Sunday. At the first cock crow, a woman dressed as I am will descend from the top of the church choir, holding a candle in her hand that she will give to you. After receiving this candle and lighting it, drip wax from it into bowls full of water and give this water to those who suffer illness and they will be healed.

Henceforth, this miracle of the Virgin was commemorated every year in May and was used to justify the foundation of a brotherhood: the Charity of Our Lady of the Ardents. We can note this connection between the Virgin and the candle on other key dates of the calendar: Candlemas (February 2) and Assumption (August 15). Through the image of the candle, the pagan myth shines through, recalling the presence of the mother goddess in the myths and rites of light.

It was customary during the month of May in the thirteenth century to honor the Virgin by building a leafy bower in her name. This

---

*[Ladies' Way is, in French, Chemin des Dames. —*Trans.*]

†[*Trouvères* is the northern French term for "troubadors." —*Trans.*]

construction made of greenery became a shrine in which her relics would be placed. The *Jeu de la Feuillée* by Adam de la Halle makes allusion to such a practice. Yet Pope Gregory, in his letter to Saint Augustine of Canterbury, suggests that this custom was purely profane. He expressed his wish that people instead "might well construct shelters of boughs for themselves around the churches that were once temples, and celebrate the solemnity with devout feasting." The literary texts of the Middle Ages often mention such lodges constructed from branches and greenery at the time of the May feasts, which demonstrates the long-standing nature of the custom. It was therefore natural that the Church would, sooner or later, take possession of the rite in order to give it a Christian patina. According to Michel Nostradamus, the pagan custom of building lodges of greenery was still quite vital in sixteenth-century Provence:

> There is an ancient custom of choosing the most beautiful young girls of the quarter, who are gorgeously outfitted with crowns of flowers, garlands, jewels, and silken adornments, and placing them on raised thrones in the guise of young goddesses set in niches. These girls are commonly called Mays to whom all passersby, on condition they be honest, are obliged to contribute a coin in return for a kiss.[9]

The ritual structure of the May festivals is nowhere more apparent than in the Christian interpretation of an old agrarian rite known as the Rogations, which Christianity has retained in its calendar in a form very much unchanged from the original.

The Rogations

The Rogations form a festive period of three days—Monday, Tuesday, and Wednesday—immediately before the Thursday feast of the Ascension. As such, the exact days of their celebration are dependent on Pascal computations. Theoretically, they move between April 28 and June 1. This was the period of the red moon, the dangerous nature of which the medieval mentality perfectly understood.

According to ecclesiastical sources, the Rogations were instituted in 470 by Saint Mamertin, the bishop of the city of Vienne in the Dauphiné region, under the name of Minor Litanies (in the liturgy the term *litany* refers to a procession that is defined by atonement and penitence). The site of Vienne in Dauphiné is known for having been an important administrative and religious center since the time of the Gauls. During the time when Christianity was established there, it became the home of the vicar of the diocese of the seven provinces of Gaul. Today, the substantial Gallo-Roman and medieval remains conserved in Vienne and Saint-Romain-en-Gal confirm the importance of this area.

The Rogations, whose roots are in this site of Vienne, could thus appear as a typically Gallic festival. In fact, the Council of Orleans (511) extended to all the churches of Gaul a celebration that appropriated the name of this festive period. In 816, Pope Leo II saw to it that this custom was formally adopted in Rome and subsequently imposed upon the entire Church.

In his *Golden Legend,* in the chapter on Rogations, Jacobus de Voragine recounts the founding of this festival:

> And this [the festival of the Rogations] was instituted by S. Mamertin, bishop of Vienne, in the time of the Emperor Leo, which reigned the year of our Lord three hundred fifty-eight . . . And is called the Lesser Litany, the Rogations and processions . . . And the cause of the institution was this: For then, at Vienne, were great earthquakes of which fell down many churches and many houses, and there were heard great sounds and great clamours by night. And then happed a terrible thing on Easter day, for fire descended from heaven that burned the king's palace. Yet happed a more marvellous thing; for like as the fiends had entered into the hogs, right so by the sufferance of God for the sins of the people, the fiends entered into wolves and other wild beasts, which every one doubted, and they went not only by the ways and by the fields, but also ran openly by the cities and devoured the children and old men and women. And when the bishop saw that every day happed such sorrowful

adventures, he commanded and ordained that the people should fast three days; and he instituted the Litanies, and then the tribulation ceased. And from thence forth, the Church hath ordained and confirmed that this Litany should be kept and observed over all.

We must note the calamities that inspired the institution of this holiday. The fire from heaven, natural catastrophes, and the invasion of demons threatened the normal cycle of fertility and posed a grave challenge to the harmonious organization of society by compromising the harvests. The festival of Rogations was therefore instituted to restore a natural order that was threatened. Jacobus de Voragine recalls the principal rite of this celebration:

Thus this Litany is called procession, for then the Church maketh general procession. And in this procession the cross is borne, the clocks and the bells are sounded and rung, the banners are borne, and in some churches a dragon with a great tail is borne. And aid and help is demanded of all saints. And the cause why the cross is borne and the bells rung is to make the evil spirits afraid and to [make them] flee.

Jacobus also points out that the ringing of bells made it possible to repel storms under any circumstances. These actions, therefore, were meant to call forth the most favorable meteorological conditions for an early harvest. Jacobus de Voragine, who here resumes the explanation of the liturgical books, reminds the reader that the Rogations were instituted "because it appeaseth the battles, that commonly begin in primetime. Second, because that the fruits which be then tender, that God will multiply. Third, because that every man should mortify in himself the movings of his flesh, which in that time boil."

Based on this testimony, the Rogations appear as a true agrarian festival. Using ambulatory rites, it involves the protection of the harvest at a critical point in the growing season, when the risks of frost have not yet disappeared and the risk of drought can be significant. Again, this is the season of the red moon, whose harmful aspects are still underscored in certain rural areas. Furthermore, red and rust are dominant mythological characteristics of the entire period of the Rogations and are at the heart of this seasonal myth. We can note, however, the guarded silence around and relative weakness of the liturgical explanation of certain details of the festival (the processional dragons and the festive triad, for example).

Robert the Devil

There can be no doubt concerning the Celtic origin of the original myth of Rogations. Existing archaeological evidence confirms that Vienne en Dauphiné was an important worship site in Gaul. Yet the wealth of remains preserved in this important city of both ancient and medieval times is not enough to reveal the secret of the myth of the Rogations. Georges Dumézil reminds us, however, that the rites performed during festivals most often have one or more purposes that are justified by one or more myths. "The periodic rites are justified by the story of an event that has occurred once and whose influence alone remains current, meaning that men can only commemorate and imitate it."[10]

The series of three days is the most visible temporal structure that makes it possible to connect the commemoration of the medieval Rogations to certain myths and stories in which this triple factor possesses a functional value. Furthermore, in the study of myths (and in the myths of festivals, *a fortiori*), it is important to pay attention to names. Myths are often passed on through names and the Rogations do not appear to be an exception to the rule. To explain the word *rogations,* we can examine the principal rite of the festival: The Litanies in fact correspond to requests (*rogare* in Latin means "to ask for"). The Litanies of this festival are presented as veritable entreaties to the saints that are invoked one after the other, with each name being followed by a response: *Ora pro nobis* (pray for us).

We cannot help but be struck by the phonetic similarity of the name Rogations and the name of the Latin festival that occurred on April 25 of the Roman calendar: Robigalia. Because the medieval Roman itinerary of the procession of Major Litanies bears a great resemblance to the ancient Roman itinerary, some linguists have jumped to the conclusion that the festival of the Rogations was a direct descendant of the festival of Robigalia. In fact, it seems rather that the word *rogations* might have been intended to erase from common memory an Indo-European name from the same family as Robigo and Robert. The fossilized myth could then be transposed and Christianized with complete impunity into the festival of the Rogations and, in certain medieval stories, such as the romance *Robert the Devil*.

Could this be the work of chance? Using an earlier calendar, we find a potential key in the commemoration of the two Roberts (April 29). We also find a Robert of Bingen celebrated on May 15 and an obscure Milanese martyr named Robustian celebrated on May 24. Rogatien and Donatien are commemorated on this same day, and this pair's association cannot help but bring to mind other sanctified couples, such as Savinien and Potentien, the first bishops of Sens, and Gervais and Protais, the Milanese martyrs. The association between Rogatien and the Rogations is as natural as the commemoration of this saint during the period of the calendar corresponding to the Minor Litanies. Could there be behind this pair of quasi-twins a reminiscence of the old myths of founding such as that of Romulus and Remus? The Rogations, Robert, and Romulus: The beginning letters provide an opportunity to recall, as Georges Dumézil does, that "for Ennius, Horace, Virgil, Propercius, Ovid, and for Cicero as for Titus-Livy and many others, Quirinus is the Roman god, the deified Roman Romulus."

Furthermore, the proximity of the date of the founding of Rome by Romulus (April 21) and that of the Robigali (April 25; associated with Quirinus-Romulus) takes us to the very heart of the Roman myth. The "theological" relation in Rome between Quirinus and Romulus also inspires the observation that the name Quirin is not rare in medieval hagiography (in addition to the Quirin, we might add Cyrin, Cyr, Cyriac, Quiriace, and so forth) and that one of the most interesting Quirins is celebrated in Lorraine on April 30, during the period preceding the Rogations. The village of Saint Quirin in the Moselle region is living testimony of an important pilgrimage that was quite vital during the Middle Ages. People went there in search of healing, for scrofulous diseases* in particular. The establishment of a Christian sanctuary on an old Gallo-Roman site perhaps demonstrated the continuity of a common memory that was, if not Roman, then at least Celtic or Indo-European.

In ancient Rome, the *flamen* of Quirinus was the official responsible for the rites relating to Robigalia. Ovid recounts the essential aspects of the ceremony in *Fastes* (Book 5, 906–32). Robigus and his consort Robigo could harm the cereal grains, for they possessed the power to cause rust, the enemy of Ceres. These terrible deities, whose feast day fell on April 25, were honored in a sacred grove on the Via Clodia, north of Rome, beyond the Milvius Bridge. The two were appeased with the immolation of a red dog, and the flamen of Quirinus invited rust (Robigo) to strike arms and armor, rather than wheat. He asked that the heavenly threat attack what was harmful to humans (the iron of weapons) rather than what was indispensable to life (the harvests).

In the medieval romance, Robert the devil is incarnated in the form of natural calamity and becomes a truly mythical force of destruction, the human scourge of humanity. He has a clear-cut predilection for rape and arson; this new Attila burns everything in his path, particularly abbeys. He tortures pilgrims and merchants, casually slaughters monks and nuns, rapes women, and even beheads the knights he defeats at tournaments. The circumstances of his conception explain his detestable nature: Robert's mother had been barren for a long time, which inspired her to turn to the devil for assistance in giving birth to a child. Her desire was satisfied, but in exchange for this service, the devil demanded the soul of the child to whom she gave birth. From his very origin, therefore, Robert is magically marked.

A very old mythological Hindu text, the Aitareya Brahmana, recounts the story of a young hero dedicated to the king of the waters, Varuna.[11]

---

*[Scrofula refers to a tuberculosis that particularly affects the lymph nodes in the neck. —*Trans.*]

King Harischandra (also known as Ambarisha) has no son, so the god Varuna offers to help him conceive a child but in return demands that this child be sacrificed. The king accepts and a son named Rohita, the red one, comes into the world. Thus, in Hindu mythology, the fate of the Varunian waters is linked to that of a red hero. The medieval Robert is clearly a red (or red-haired) figure originally connected with the rust of the Rogations. His myth partially matches that of the red-haired man that has existed throughout the imaginal realm of the Western world into the present day. The folktale known as *The Little Gardener with the Golden Hair* has perpetuated this motif in popular tradition and confirms the magical nature of this uncommon hero who possesses a clear line of descent from the mythical figure.

The Dragons and the Wasteland

The medieval Varunian hero exercises a destructive power that is comparable to that of the goddess Robigo. Yet at the end of the medieval romance, this figure radically changes function and plays the role of the providential warrior who repels assailants on three occasions. It should not be forgotten that during the three days of the Rogations, people paraded about with the figure of a dragon with a long tail. This creature actually embodies the tricephalic one, the monster that holds back the waters, a figure of Indo-European mythology whose importance has been underscored by Georges Dumézil.

Another detail of the romance is quite interesting if we compare it to a detail in *The Story of the Grail*. Robert is wounded during the second attack he is forced to suffer; an iron spearhead pierces his thigh and remains there until he manages to conceal himself and safely remove his armor. At this point he finds himself close to a mysterious fountain near which there are apparitions (or a celestial messenger) who give him magical weapons each day. After pulling the iron spear from his leg, he hides it underground in one of the fountain's springs. The deadly iron point and the wound on the leg call to mind the dolorous blow inflicted on the Fisher King in the Grail story. In his study of the various versions of this dolorous blow in the Arthurian legend, Jean Marx underscores perfectly the link established between the cursed iron (rust and blood-covered, for rust could be considered the blood of iron) and the Wasteland, the precise curse that the rites of the Rogations seek to exorcise.

In *Balain* (a thirteenth-century Arthurian romance in prose), Garlan, the Red Knight, inflicts the dolorous blow on Balain, and this wound immediately casts three kingdoms into "misery and mourning" for thirty-two years. Related to this, in the oldest Celtic tradition, the wounding of the king brings about the sterility of his entire kingdom.

Finally, the romance *Robert the Devil* contains a mysterious name that has escaped the notice of mythologists. When he finally reaches the last stage of his contrition, Robert wants to convert, and the pope sends him to a forest close to Rome: "To the forest that is large and vast / Which has for name Marabonde" (verses 639–40).

In this quasi-fairylike place where a handsome hermitage is located, a *moult bele fontaine* (beautiful fountain) can be seen. If we break down the name of Marabonde into *mar-* and *abonde,* we can recognize in the second half of the word the name of a magical creature from *The Romance of the Rose* who governs the nocturnal ridings of those who "think themselves to be witches wandering the night with Dame Habonde."

In his *De Universo,* Guillaume d'Auvergne defines the name Habonde as "abundance"; in Latin *abundans* is the present participle of *abundo,* "which overflows" (as in water). Therefore, by way of Habonde, the fertilizing waters of the Rogations would have a natural relation to Robert, the key figure in the Indo-European myth that preceded the medieval Rogations. We can note, incidentally, that the name Habonde has not completely vanished from popular memory; there is a place named Abundance in the Upper Savoy area and an Abondant in the Eure-et-Loir region.

The curse of the Wasteland (devastated by a mysterious sterility or a divine calamity) that haunts the entire Grail legend seems connected to an old seasonal myth, which we can better analyze and understand in view of the rites and myth of the Rogations. Like Indra, it is Perceval's

Fig. 6.1 Saint George

task to assume the role of the civilizing hero who enables the world to escape the inevitability of a Wasteland, with all the attendant symbolism of that term. It is the great hero Indra in the Hindu texts who transfixes the dragon that holds the waters captive and who digs the riverbeds that will carry water to all of humanity. This return of fertility permits the world to survive the chaos that a universal drought would surely have created: "Indra has fertilized the young women and they rejoice like springs that have just burst through the ground; the young, respectable brides who were slowly languishing, he fertilized them. He has satisfied the thirst of the parched fields and prairies. Henceforth, they will have a husband that can perform miracles."

The dragon that appears in the myth of Indra is akin to that carried in procession in the Middle Ages during the Rogations under the names the gargoyle of Rouen (slain by Saint Romain), the *graouilli** of Metz,[12] the "salted flesh" dragon of Troyes, the dee drake of Montlhéry, and a good many others. It is the same dragon that swallowed up all the waters, one of the many forms assumed by the pre-Christian god, which

---

*[The graouilli is a duck-beaked dragon whose name derives from the German word *graülich*, meaning "terrifying." —*Trans.*]

the Church sought to exorcise with the Rogations in order to incorporate an imaginal element of fertility that it had felt it had been lacking. In medieval Christianity, the hero and monster slayer is often a bishop and sometimes a soldier (for example, Saint George, whose feast day falls on April 23).

The traditional May festivals reinstate this simultaneously mythical and ritual context of the battle of the seasons. In May we find the pivotal moments of the calendar, for this is the time when the Wild Woman can heap the world of men with her riches or saddle humanity with all the dangers that threaten the fertility of the world.

SEVEN

Saint John's Day

The summer feast of Saint John corresponds with one of the year's two solstice periods. It is not by chance that John's name is associated with this key moment of the annual cycle. In Roman antiquity, Janus was the god of doors (*janua* in Latin). Thus his patronage of places of passage, doors, and thresholds made him particularly suited to overseeing the transitional moments of the year. The first month of the year (January is *januarius* in Latin) was naturally dedicated to him.

Of course, the name Janus was reworked in the Middle Ages. It was rewritten as the biblical name John and thereby introduced a Christian allegory beneath the cosmic mechanism of the solstices. Saint John the Baptist, the last prophet of the Hebrew scriptures, announced the coming of Christ, proclaiming that he would be condemned to wane when Christ was born in his own divinity. Fittingly, the birth of John the Baptist is celebrated around the summer solstice (June 24), when the sun begins to wane, whereas that of Christ is celebrated during the winter solstice (December 25), when the sun has begun to grow stronger again.

June 24 is the gateway to midsummer, whereas December 27 (the feast day of Saint John the Evangelist) ensures the transition into winter. The two festivals to two Johns thus constitute two pivotal points in the year. In fact, in these two Johns, the Christian Middle Ages reinterpreted the pre-Christian figure of Janus *bifrons* (the two-faced Janus) in which we can also see the wild Merlin, who could be at the same time a child

Fig. 7.1. Saint John the Baptist

and an old man, very young and very old. Traditionally, Merlin could look in the two opposing directions of time simultaneously because he escaped the ordinary constraints of time and because he, too, was a prophet, much like John the Baptist.

The Fires of Saint John

The fires of Saint John remain the most vivid evidence of a pre-Christian tradition attached to the summer solstice. The bonfire of Saint John echoes other fires or fire festivals that occur at other times of the year—for instance, the bonfire of Carnival, which allows for the burning of the giant mannequin condemned to vanish before Lent; and the fire of Easter, which has been preserved in the tradition of the Pascal candle and the distinctive fire known as the Judas fire, which is lit on Easter eve and is fueled by boxwood. Other examples are the fire of Beltane, lit on the eve of May 1, Walpurgis Night; the fire of Hogunna, lit on the eve of All Saints' Day; and the fire on December 25 that consumes the Yule log—all of which speak to the same primordial rite of celebration and exorcism.

The fires of Saint John (or Jouannés) were kindled during the evening of June 23, the eve of the feast day itself. The bonfire was generally built around a tree from which all branches had been pruned, forming a kind of central "maypole." This pole was decorated with crowns of flowers that would later be used to protect the local inhabitants' homes from begin struck by lightning. The lighting of the fire sometimes took on a liturgical tone: A procession walked from the church to the bonfire site, which the priest would bless before the blaze was set. The actual rite of lighting, however, more often retained its profane character. In Paris during the time of the Ancien Régime* it was tradition that the king of France should personally light this fire: Louis XI, Henri II, and even Louis XIV respected this custom. Once the fire started crackling, circle dances formed and people sang and danced until the flames were extinguished. In his seventh canto of *Mireille,* Frédéric Mistral lauded the enthusiasm of the young people who "three times showed their bravado with great leaps through the flames." The most agile jumped above the hot coals to win a year of health and happiness or the benefit of a good omen for a coming marriage.

These pyres and bonfires, however, sometimes served as the framework for much less friendly forms of amusement. One custom demanded that a number of animals deemed harmful—cats, foxes, toads, vipers, and so forth—be sealed up alive in a sack, which was hung above the fire until the animals burned to death. This sacrifice was believed to dispel bad luck. The specific animals sacrificed varied by region: Snakes were sacrificed in Luchon, cats in Gap and Metz, horses in Thuringia and Lyon, bulls in Savoy, and wolves in Jumièges. Sometimes people burned simply the bones of dead animals to drive away ghosts. One legend explains this cruel custom of burning alive certain animals: A terrible epidemic raged in a city when a knight claimed to have seen the devil in the shape of a cat and sought to kill it. Once he drew his sword, however, the devil cat vanished with a howl and the epidemic

---

*[This term refers to the French social system of three orders that prevailed until the French Revolution. —*Trans.*]

disappeared with it. It was concluded that the cat was responsible for the plague, and to exorcise the threat of any future illness, henceforth thirteen cats were burned in the public square every year.

The cat's bad reputation has persisted through time, with some believing it to hold the soul of a witch or even the devil himself. In 1233, the Dominican inquisitor Etienne de Bourbon described how a woman named Bérengère from Fanjeaux in the Aude region attended a summoning of the devil performed by Saint Dominic in 1206. It seems the saint forced the devil to appear in the form of a black cat before nine heretical and somewhat witchlike women of Fanjeaux. The ritual massacre of cats (or other animals deemed diabolic) on Saint John's Day can be placed in the context of such exorcism practices.

In his *Golden Legend,* Jacobus de Voragine pursues this explanation of exorcism to justify the fire ritual. According to him, it is necessary to exterminate on Saint John's Day the dragons that flew through the sky, for they were particularly active during this time of the year, which witnessed the return of warm temperatures. Because these dragons (or demons) posed a heavy threat to the fertility of the earth and the circulation of water, their malignant influence had to be diverted by maintaining nauseating fires. This speaks of ancient belief in revenants and Otherworld beings that periodically threaten the human world with death and destruction.

It is quite obvious that Saint John's Day in the summer, like Candlemas or Christmas, had its own revenants. There is, for example, the Green Wolf, well known in the town of Jumièges, whose manifestations are just as dreadful as those of the bear at Candlemas. Similarly, Saint John's Day is one of the eight annual dates during which the Wild One makes an appearance. This Wild One can take on various guises (that of a cat, wolf, bear, and so on) but beneath its animal disguise, it is always the same pagan deity. Stories concerning werewolves can be viewed in the context of this divine and initiatory metempsychosis.[1]

The Christianization of the solstice period of Saint John's Day was carried out by means of a biblical figure who presents some fairly significant features of wildness. John the Baptist corresponds, in fact, to the one picture of the Wild Man as he was imagined in the Middle Ages. According to the evangelist Matthew, John the Baptist wore "a raiment of wild camel hide and a leather girdle around his loins; his food was locusts and wild honey." There could be no better description of this figure's association with the wild life, but he is not the model for all the Wild Men of the Middle Ages, for some of these possessed specific and relatively unvarying features that do not derive in any way from the biblical John but rather come from an Indo-European archetype. Yet because the Bible offered a figure who bore an astonishing resemblance to the pagan figures of the Wild Man that the Church sought to conceal, Christianity had no trouble using the image of Saint John the Baptist to cover the one paganism had bequeathed from its archaic memory banks: the all-powerful deity of the Otherworld who rules over life and death and organizes the cycles of time.

The Church fought vigorously against the archetype of the Wild Man because it fed into pagan beliefs in metempsychosis: The Celtic deities were believed to reincarnate into certain animals, and Julius Caesar observed during the Gallic Wars that the Gallic druids considered the transmigration of souls a fundamental dogma of their religion:

> They wish to inculcate this as one of their leading tenets that souls do not become extinct but instead pass after death from one body to another, and they think that by this tenet men are to a great degree excited to valor, the fear of death being disregarded. They likewise discuss and impart to the youth many things respecting the stars and their motion . . .[2]

Christianity theologically denied this concept was thus compelled to fight it and relegate it to heresy. Yet this early belief in the transmigration of souls into animals still survives in certain universal folktales and goes a long way toward explaining the fantasy of the werewolf and shedding light on certain aspects of witchcraft in which the black cat is considered a witch or the goat is thought to wear the face of the god of the Otherworld.

One figure of folklore assumes both the mythic legacy associated with the ancient figure of the Wild Man and a Christian interpretation: Jean de l'Ours (John the Bear).[3] From his ursine father he inherited the power to gain access to the world below, from which he returned with a wife and a fortune after sacrificing his thigh. Jean de l'Ours was also faced with a problem that required him to enter the Otherworld. His name, shared with that of John the Baptist, points to the fact that the "wild" Baptist recalls this mythic interpretation of the Wild Man.

The Sacred Stone

Saint Peter the Apostle is celebrated on June 29, five days after Saint John's Day. Peter's name recalls the word *stone*,* suggesting obvious mythological extensions, especially those related to the Celtic and pre-Celtic world. The Bible explicitly recalls this connection between Peter and the stone in Christ's declaration: "You are Peter and on this rock I will build my Church." This symbolic connection between the apostle Peter and the rock, seemingly established from a simple play on words, was certainly exploited by the Church at the time it was converting pagans to Christianity, for yet again a saint is used to Christianize rites that are not at all Christian or biblical in nature.

The name Peter could be a remnant of the megalithic cult stones and dolmens that are often connected to solstice rites. It is known that churches dedicated to Saint Peter were built on ancient megalithic sites. It is logical that ancient druidic stones would be enveloped in a Christian cult by means of Saint Peter or other saints associated with him through the calendar. In the Middle Ages, this was the case in Lyon, where the stone of Saint Pothin was honored during the summer solstice. Saint Pothin's festival is celebrated in June several days before that of Saint Peter.

The Church's battle against the pagan worship of stones was particularly long and difficult. The twentieth canon of the Council of Nantes

---

*[The Latin word for stone is *petra*. The connection is much more apparent in French, in which the same word, *pierre*, is both the proper name Peter and "stone." —*Trans.*]

(658) ordered the overturning or burial of the megalithic stones worshipped by the pagans. This prescription could not have been applied successfully everywhere, for in certain regions even in the nineteenth century the same superstitious practices devoted to the stones could still be found.

We can certainly follow the fifth- and sixth-century worship of stones by the people of Gaul who had not been completely uprooted from their pagan practices.[4] In fact, the twenty-third canon of the Council of Arles (between 443 and 452) condemns those who, "on the territory of any bishop, either light the small torches or worship the trees, the springs, or the stones." A capitulary of King Childebert I (511–58) offers criticism of those who, despite certain warnings, have not immediately cast down standing stones or idols in their region that have been consecrated to the demon. In 567, the twenty-third canon of the Council of Tours repeats: "Let all those who appear to persist in their folly of performing around any stones, trees, or fountains, manifest sites of paganism, acts that are incompatible with the rules of the Church, be driven from the Holy Church and let none permit them to approach the holy altar."* In 789 a "general warning" specified: "With respect to the trees or stones or fountains, where several fools light fires or perform other practices, we command in the most express manner that this custom, the worst of all and detestable to God, be extirpated and destroyed wherever it may be encountered."

We can note a universal condemnation of both stones and the fires lit near these stones. Interestingly, however, in Lyon the worship of stones was connected to the fires of Saint John.[5] The cult dedicated to the stone of Saint Pothin is evidence of this Christian–pagan connection: A pilgrimage leaving every year from the chapel of Saint Pierre de Vase to the Church of Saint Nizier, which once bore the name Saint Pierre, had as its final objective the stone of Saint Pothin. According to legend, this stone supported the head of the first bishop of Lyon when he was suffering in prison. In this we can recognize the stone pillow motif that

---

*[To "approach the holy altar" is to take part in Holy Communion. —*Trans.*]

is so widespread in folklore, which is well corroborated in Celtic tradition in the seventh-century *Life of Saint Columban,* which tells how this saint slept on bare rock with only a stone for a pillow.[6] The stone of Saint Pothin was, like all stone pillows, a Celtic (or pre-Celtic) megalith that had miraculously survived attacks by both Roman bureaucrats and Christian priests. It can certainly be described as a true stone of worship. Well before the time of Christianity, people visited its site to obtain health and fertility.

Another rite was also linked to stones at the time of the summer solstice: the rite of the Holy Vinage—that is, the water that is said to miraculously change into wine on Saint John's Day. In certain regions, people visit a Saint John spring to drink this water transformed into wine, which is said to increase fertility. The beverage was often a ruddy-colored water into which were dipped the relics of Saint John or another saint. In Embrum, this drink was produced by scraping the stone of Saint Foutin, another name for Pothin. The phallic significance of this rite is beyond doubt, especially when we consider the name of Foutin who entered Paradise.* The cult stone resembled the phallus of a fertility god, and to ingest its substance was to obtain a personal guarantee of fertility.

On this point, as on so many others, the Church was forced to tolerate ancestral practices that quite obviously had no Christian basis. Furthermore, the Chrisitianization of these cult stones remained rudimentary for the most part, incorporating into their rites a procession followed by a blessing. Indeed, the Church appeared defenseless against the persistence of these beliefs in the mentalities of the people among whom it was evangelizing. It therefore determined to take action against the pagan rite by encouraging the legends of pious individuals associated with these pagan stones. Similarly, the Church took pains to create an artificial but likely connection between martyrs and the stones that had never been touched by these individuals.

---

*[The name Foutin is reminiscent of the French word *foutre,* which is used as a vulgar expression for sexual intercourse. —*Trans.*]

Pilgrimages were most often presented as exorcism either of the diabolical invasion of paganism or of situations that threatened the entire society (drought, epidemics, and so forth). Using specific rites, the pilgrimage was intended to occupy a territory that had earlier been held by malevolent powers. The practice of the most common pilgrimages consisted of parading simulacra—the statues of saints that had been found to have once depicted pagan deities or animals—over perfectly circumscribed itineraries. It is significant that paganism was fought using a rite borrowed from paganism itself. Article 28 of the *Indiculus superstitionum et paganarium,* a kind of inventory of pagan superstitions written during the eleventh century, explains the custom of carrying simulacra through the countryside (*De simulacro quod per campos portant*). Among the rites intended to fight drought were processions of statues representing both male and female saints. As we have seen, the *Life of Saint Martin* by Sulpicius Severus indirectly makes mention of this custom in the fifth century. Moreover, this hagiographic text reveals the reality of a belief in simulacra even as it sought to minimize its importance.

The Solstice Madness

The summer solstice appeared in medieval rites as a particularly ominous and dangerous period. In the middle of the seventh century, a *Life of Saint Eligius* denounces all those who, during the feast of Saint John, "celebrate the solstices and perform dances in circles or with leaping (*aut vallationes aut saltationes*) and diabolical carols or songs (*aut caraulas aut cantica diabolica*)." These prohibitions suggest that such practices were widespread in the seventh century and that the Church was seeking to stamp them out once and for all. Yet it seems to have had a great deal of difficulty meeting this goal, if we believe the chronicle.

Here again, reality and myth appear to commingle. While history has preserved several tales of cursed dances, it is often quite hard to believe in the substance of the facts recorded. In any event, in certain manifestations of collective and irrepressible dancing—dancing "epidemics"—the names Saint John's dance (related to Saint John's disease, a form of epilepsy), Saint Vitus's dance, and Saint Guy's dance come up again and again. Incidentally, all these saints are commemorated within several calendar days of each other: June 24 is Saint John's Day and June 15 is both Saint Vitus's Day and Saint Guy's Day, and all fall during the solstice time that prompted these ritual dances, suggestive of the fact that they are connected to the same mythical context. The Church denounced these irrepressible dances as phenomena of possession and strove to establish parades to replace these "manipulations of the devil." It believed that processions, pilgrimages, and the worship of healing saints would form a bulwark against the diabolical madness of the solstice and restore more serenity and piety to overheated minds.

In fact, the night of Saint John, like May 1, had a very bad reputation. A symphonic poem by Mussorgsky constructed out of ancient Russian tales provides the musical evocation of a sabbath on "bald mountain."* It includes: "Underground rumor of supernatural voices. The appearance of the spirits of darkness, followed by those of the god Chernobog. Glorification of the dark god. Black Mass. The witches' Sabbath is interrupted by the far away tolling of the bell of a small village church. The spirits of darkness scatter. Daybreak."

Saint John's night was one of the privileged moments of the year when the witches held their Sabbath, preparing abominable feasts in which the theme of cannibalism was predominant. Their preferred dish was said to be the flesh of unbaptized infants combined with toad skin and served with a blood sauce. Witches' Sabbaths were generally held on the ancient sites of pagan worship. Such "bald mountains" (mountains with a bare top) survive in French place-names such as Chaumont and Montceau.† The "baldness" to which they testify reflects an old mythic inevitability that also appears in certain Grail romances: the theme of the Wasteland, or land that is sterile or cursed. In general, such a site

---

*[This is commonly known as "Night on Bald Mountain," but was actually called "St. John's Night on the Bare Mountain" (Ivanova noch' na Lisoy gore) and was supposed to have been originally inspired by a short story by Gogol. —*Ed.*]

†[*Cheau* means "bald" in French. —*Trans.*]

is marked by the presence of fairies and can be saved only by a human sacrifice. The bald mountain was naturally transformed into a place of abomination and savagery when it had not been taken in hand by the divine redemption of a saint. It was a site associated with a fairy who degenerated into practicing satanism.

Christianity connected Saint John's night to the idea of dangerous magic because of the feast day's association with ancestral rites over which the Church had no control. Shakespeare's *A Midsummer Night's Dream,* for instance, testifies to this, as does Henrik Ibsen's nineteenth-century dramatic play entitled *Saint John's Night.*

Women and, after a certain era, witches had a favorite occupation during this fateful night: the picking of malefic herbs. In fact, the herbs of Saint John were as well known as the fires that bore his name and were no doubt the focal point for an old magic, probably of druidic origin, that has been perpetuated in folklore traditions. We can note that the love philter manufactured for Tristan and Iseult—a beverage composed of magical herbs that drove the lovers to an amorous madness—was drunk on the day of Saint John.[7] The reputation generally attached to the herbs of Saint John is that they can either cause or cure madness. Thus the young Blaise Pascal, whom people claimed was enchanted by the wizard Piarrone, had to ingest as his cure a "Saint John's bouillon" consisting of herbs culled during the night of June 23 into June 24. Indeed, this festival was enveloped for a very long time with a dangerous magic associated with every form of madness.

The efforts to Christianize Saint John's Day were in vain. In fact, there is a core of pagan myths and beliefs at the heart of Saint John's Day that the Church had a great deal of trouble dispelling. Bishop Burchard of Worms denounced very early on the riding of Diana:

> . . . that superstition which these villainous women claim to perform, these women who are Satan's fiends and minions and are deceived by diabolical fantasies. With Diana, the pagan goddess, and in the company of a host of other women, they ride animals and travel great distances during the silence of the middle of the

night, obeying the orders of their mistress, Diana, and placing themselves at her service on specific predetermined nights.[8]

Even if the bishop does not explicitly mention the nights to which he refers, it is easy to see to which periods of the year he alludes. We can certainly have no illusions concerning the Latin name Diana: It is the clerical name of a deity belonging to the Celtic world and was used in Church writings as a kind of code name for fairy. Under the name Diana, Burchard probably noted the syllable *ana,* which he compared with the word *ane,* meaning "duck," the bird-woman of Celtic myths, which evokes the riding of birds in the sky. He also may well have heeded the approximate etymology that compares the name Diana with Janus (and therefore with Saint John). Victor Hugo recalls this in his *Choses vues* (Things Seen) of August 18, 1846: "Janus depicts the sun as Diana does the moon. It is the same sound and the same word—Janus, Jana, Djana, Diana, according to some, Dia = dea Jana = Diana."

Burchard's testimony is interesting in more than one respect because it provides corroboration of eleventh-century beliefs that would later lead to witches' death at the stake. These aerial rides in the company of Diana bring to mind witches who fly through the air on their brooms—a proper sign of satanic madness. His words also allow us to recall that the practices of witches contained irreducible elements of pre-Christian paganism (quite often of Celtic origin) that Christianity was incapable of incorporating. This aerial ride is directly reminiscent of that of the Mesnie Hellequin, whose mythic character we have already examined. As historians of religion have noted, the Inquisition incorporated sorcery into heresy and exterminated witches with the same relentless obstinacy it displayed against heretics. In reality, heresy and witchcraft are only two aspects of the same cultural reality involving the mythic forms and themes of Celtic paganism that in some cases were raised to a sacral status by the Church.

Behind the majority of rites related to sorcery are hidden practices that have a connection with the beliefs of the carnivalesque "religion." The cannibalistic meal of the witches is an extreme example of the rites of a Carnival feast consisting of an abundance of meat dishes. The witches broom turned straw-side up and equipped with a candle can be linked to the brands (torches) of Carnival. In fact, during Carnival people carried torches that were quite often brooms that had been set alight. The fear inspired by witches is akin to that inspired by werewolves, vampires, will-o'-the-wisps, and other mythical creatures—and witches covered by bearskins or wolf hides took on the appearance of the revenants of Carnival. Finally, the worship of the goat is found in both Celtic (and carnivalesque) folklore and witchcraft. During the trial of Abel de la Rue cited by Bodin in the 1587 edition of his *Démonomanie des sorcier,* the defendant declared that "having danced for close to two quarters of an hour, all fell to their knees, and the stated master Pierre would have told him the time had come to worship the goat, and that this was the Devil and the one to whom he had promised to show honor and reverence." Every year, in Killorgin in Kerry County, Ireland, a goat wrapped in garlands of flowers and placed firmly on a decorated throne is paraded through the area. This animal, which plays a major role in many Sabbaths, first and foremost appears as the reincarnation of the horned Celtic god Cernunnos, the counterpart to the fatted cow or bull of Carnival.

Looking in parts and pieces at these facts prevents us from perceiving their symbolic consistency, yet the testimony provided by medieval literature reveals their imaginal relationships.

The Wheel of Fire

In the *Life of Saint Vincent of Agen* there is mentioned a pagan cult dedicated to a wheel of fire. Saint Vincent is celebrated on June 9, a date that is significant because of its proximity to the solstice. During Saint John's night in the Lorraine region, an ancestral custom allowed for the annual reappearance of a wheel of fire that might well be a remote testament to a mythic tradition: A large, flaming wheel was sent rolling down the slope of the hill that overlooks Sierck-les-Bains in Moselle. If it had been launched correctly, this wheel finished its journey in the waters of the Moselle River. Made largely of straw, the wheel was meant to roll as far as possible. If it fell into the Moselle, it foretold an excellent wine harvest for the year. All the villagers were expected to provide straw for the manufacture of the wheel, and those who dared refuse could expect to see the animals in their stables catch Saint Guy's dance. No myth appears to support this Moselle-area rite; perhaps it disappeared during the passage of time. On the other hand, this practice has been quite faithfully maintained even today in various regions.

In a study of Scythian rites and myths, however, Georges Dumézil unearthed a myth that may relate to this rite. In the Caucasus region he found practices identical to this Moselle custom that are related to the myth of a hero named Soslan who suffers mutilation caused by a solar wheel. Before his birth, a shepherd fell in love with the beautiful Setanta, but could not be with her because they were separated by a river. He therefore projected his semen over the river to the stone on which Setanta sat. The young girl took the stone with her and, through the intervention of the smith of the Nartes, gave birth nine months later to the boy named Soslan. In order to make the child invincible, the smith dipped the newborn child in a bath with the help of a pair of pliers. But at his knees, the places where the pliers gripped him, the child was not invulnerable. As an adult, Soslan's mortal enemy was Syrdon, who was prepared to do whatever necessary to slay Soslan. This nemesis fulfilled his wish by appealing to a divine entity that sent him a thinking machine: the Wheel of Balsaeg (or Marsaeg), a cutting wheel that sliced Soslan's knee and brought about the hero's death.

Caucasian variants of this same myth also incorporate a snakelike monster with the head of a giant who seeks to steal seed. This detail suggests the seasonal nature of the myth, which relates to the fertility cycle.

The image of this mythical wheel can also be found in Gallo-Roman statuary in the figure of the anguipede, a giant whose body ends in a fish tail.* Quite often Jupiter on horseback, who prevails over the Gallic god/anguipede, carries a bolt of lightning in his hand. In fact, the wheel and the bolt of lightning appear to be interchangeable; the wheel could well

*[This giant is often known as the giant of the wheel. —*Trans.*]

be a symbol for lightning. On an altar dedicated to Jupiter unearthed in the Narbonnaise region, a wheel is depicted with the term FULGAR. The association of the wheel with the lightning bolt goes back to the oldest Indo-European mythology: A text from the *Mahabharata* mentions a wheel that spits lightning bolts when it turns, and Agni provided Vishnu with a "wheel with a bolt of lightning" to help him fight Arjuna.

The Wheel of Fortune

A fourteenth-century manuscript of *The Romance of Fauvel* contains a detail of great importance in the study of the Mesnie Hellequin and in the analysis of the mythic wheel associated with Saint John's Day.

The passage opens with a description of Paris and some lamentations. How could it be that such a beautiful city is in the hands of Fauvel [Favel], the treacherous horse? Fauvel decides to convoke his court, which, allegorically, is composed of all the vices and sins in the world. Following a sumptuous feast, the horse leaves to sleep with his wife, but the couple are awakened by a horrible *chalivali* orchestrated by the Mesnie Hellequin in the streets and at the crossroads of the city.

> Disguises there were in great variety. Some wore their clothing inside out or backward; others had adorned themselves with large sacks and the robes of monks. They could hardly be recognized, so done up and undone were they. They thought only of wrongdoing: One was holding a large cauldron; the other a hook, a grill, and a pestle; and another a copper pot. All were pretending to be drunk.

These figures cause a huge din—drums and cowbells, cymbals and sleighbells—and they pull a cart that holds a machine with wheels:

> They all were leading a cart. And in this cart was a machine with tumbril wheels, which were quite strong, stiff, and well crafted. When turning, they would hit six iron bars that were nailed quite firmly to the hub. Just listen! Such a loud noise and of such great

variety, so ugly and dreadful made by knocking things together that even thunder could not make itself heard over it. They were making such a hubbub that nothing like it has ever been heard before. One was exposing his ass, the other was tearing down an awning. One was breaking windows, another was salting wells, and another was throwing shit in people's faces. They were extremely ugly and quite wild. Their faces were adorned with false beards; they were carrying two caskets . . . There was a large giant that went ahead, howling at the top of his lungs. He was clad in buskin. I believe he was Hellequin in the company of all his folk.[9]

The giant Hellequin's parade includes a funeral cart with a particularly squeaky wheel. Added to the howls of Hellequin's creatures, the noise created by this wheel is intolerable. It freezes with terror all those who hear it because it is a sinister omen.

The Celtic model for this wheeled machine could well be the "wheel with oars" (*roth ramhach*) that appears in medieval Irish literature. This is a ship that holds a thousand beds, with each bed holding a thousand men. The vessel travels on both land and sea and is associated with a Saint John's Day festival that is said to fall on a Friday.

The systematic association of the wheel with Saint John's Day is confirmed by numerous testimonies from the Middle Ages.[10] An anonymous English author, cited by the folklorist van Gennep, denounced the pagan rites of Saint John's Day and most particularly a wheel that was rolled during the festival. In 1165, the liturgist Jean Beleth described the nocturnal corteges of Saint John's Day, during which people paraded with brands and torches as well as with a blazing wheel. Guillaume Durant, another liturgist, of the thirteenth century, analyzed the meaning of the Saint John's wheel by stressing its similarity to the sun and its course, which reaches its apogee before starting to decline at the moment of the summer solstice. Finally, during the festival of Gayant, celebrated in Douai on the third Sunday in June, a large wheel of fortune holding several mannequins symbolizing the various social classes was paraded in a procession. The giant (Gayant), the key figure in the calendar of Carnival, is thus connected to the Saint John's wheel that formerly symbolized Gayant's power over the storm or the lives of men and which became a reduced image of the entire world. In this way, the mythical wheel of the summer solstice gradually took on an allegorical significance and became part of a new myth that attempted to fit in with a Christian vision of the world.

The wheel of the solstice transformed into the wheel of life and the Wheel of Fortune, a morphing that revealed the stakes of Saint John's Day, to which this wheel is so closely linked. In it, an implicit comparison is established between the cycle of the year and the evolution of human life that goes through ups and downs, luck and misfortune. This new symbolism of the Wheel of Fortune was especially developed in the didactic literature of the Middle Ages, which tended to overlay a rite connected to an archaic myth with a moral and abstract meaning. Religious thinking took possession of the symbol and projected upon it an image of the vicissitudes of human life. The Wheel of Fortune thus became the image of the vanities of the world or the fragility of human life. The same fateful value was attached to Saint John's Day before its Christianization. This festival acknowledged every danger of the fairies (in other words, the Fates), whose secret dream has always been to force humans to do their will.

EIGHT
August 1, Lughnasa

The earth became so hot that it started to sweat
so much it created the sea, and this is why the sea is salty.

RABELAIS, *PANTAGRUEL,* CHAPTER 2

Forty days after the fires of Saint John's Day begins the canicular period.* In the ancient Celtic calendar, August 1, a day in this period, coincided with the feast of Lughnasa.[1] During antiquity and the Middle Ages, the canicular days (from around mid-July to mid-August) not only corresponded to a period when hot weather prevailed, but also carried a set of mythical beliefs associating the heat with a cosmic threat bordering on cataclysm: The world was truly under threat of an apocalyptic end by fire during these dates. The dog days were the preeminent period of devastating monsters who must be fought by extraordinary heroes and saints. The seasonal nature of this battle cannot be overlooked, for it explains in large part many of the profane or hagiographic themes that illustrate the mythical canicular season.

Canicular Heroes and Monsters

The ancient Romans lived in dread of the canicular days and sought to avoid any harmful extremes of the period by immolating a red dog

---

*[The canicular period is popularly known as the dog days. —*Trans.*]

dedicated to Sirius. This star bears the name Canicule in the constellation of the Dog (*canis* in Latin, with its diminutive form, "little dog," being *caniculum*). One further connection is that Sirius is associated with the hunter Orion, a key figure in the Greek canicular myths.

Among the significant canicular figures of medieval mythology, we can single out the knight of the lion, Yvain, who performs a rite intended to make rain near a boiling spring, the fountain of Barenton. According to the myth, by pouring a little water on this stormy fountain, it is possible to unleash a terrible tempest that would be particularly welcome during a time of drought. In the course of his adventures, Yvain meets a lion, the living emblem of his knightly ardor and courage and also the privileged face of a royal figure. The lion (Leo) appears as a zodiac symbol of the hottest time of the year (July 22–August 23). This identifies Yvain as a canicular hero: a king of the weather.

In the Spanish adaptation of *The Quest of the Holy Grail,* Galahad, son of Lancelot, deals a death wound to a barking beast* that lives in a lake.[2] Since this beast began haunting this lake, its water boiled like the water at Barenton. This fairy monster possesses obvious canine characteristics, and that it barks betrays its connection to the canicular world. The mythical origin of this baying beast can be found in the animals of the Wild Hunt.

Among the canicular figures of the Middle Ages, we should also take special note of Tristan, who is generally accompanied by a dog, who does not simply provide him with assistance during the interminable hunting parties, but is also the veritable emblem of the hero. Just as Yvain was considered the knight of the lion, Tristan was the knight of the dog. In fact, the hero's dog is not merely his friendly companion or a simple novelistic device employed as the pretext for more or less secondary episodes in the hero's tale; he actually defines Tristan mythologically as a sacred figure, a great monster slayer and the founder of civilized order as opposed to monstrous chaos.

---

*[The "baying beast" is the more literal translation of the monster normally referred to in the Arthurian Cycle as the Questing Beast. —*Trans.*]

There is little difference between a knight of the lion and a knight of the dog. Yvain's lion behaves in a way comparable to Béroul's canine "hero." In other words, the story of Tristan and that of Yvain are connected to the same archetypal myth of the dog days (canicule). Like Tristan, Yvain confronts monstrous creatures and assumes an authentic stature as a civilizing hero.

The exploits of King Arthur are perhaps not be as well known in this regard, but they have their origin in the same mythological vein. Before one of his more splendid deeds, Arthur experiences a strange dream:

> It seemed to him, from where he lay sleeping, that a bear had flown toward him through the air. The creature came from the east and was quite ugly, and fat and was very large and great. It was a horrible creature. Facing him was a dragon who had come flying out of the west; flames shot from its eyes. This dragon and the light he gave off illuminated all the surrounding land and sea. The dragon attacked the bear, but the latter beast put up an energetic defense. The dragon encircled the bear and finally managed to beat it to the ground.

In this dream, Arthur, son of Uther Pendragon, is obviously designated by the dragon, but who is his adversary, the flying bear? To truly grasp the meaning of this dream, we must return it to its natural context. It in fact heralds the episode that follows it: A terrible giant has kidnapped Helen, niece of King Hoël of Spain (himself a nephew of King Arthur), and carries her off to Mont-Saint-Michel, where he subjects her to terrible sexual abuses. The "too tender" young girl cannot support this assault and dies. Arthur must avenge her by confronting the giant. Following a terrible combat, he manages to kill the bear-giant and thus the prophecy in the dream is fulfilled.

The flying bear (in other words, the bear-bird) is another shape assumed by the canicular monster, bringing to mind the giant of the Mesnie Hellequin and merging into the countless dragons that Christian saints have confronted individually. The tales of heroic initiation inserted into medieval literary texts fully reveal their suspect mythological ancestry. The Christian Middle Ages would draw from the same mythological sources to recount the legends of the saints, who were also called upon to confront monsters that had become obvious allegorical symbols of paganism.

With respect to Saint Dominic (celebrated on August 4), *The Golden Legend* tells how, before his birth, his mother saw in a dream that she was carrying in her womb a small dog holding in its mouth a lit torch that would light the entire world. Once he was born, close to the baptismal fonts there could be seen on little Dominic's forehead a shining star that illuminated the whole land. The two motifs of the dog and the star associated with Dominic become readily explicable when we take into account the canicular context of his birth. Furthermore, Dominic is the founder of the Domincan Order, which sometimes presents its members as *Domini canes,* the "hounds of God."

July 29, Saint Martha's Day and the Tarasque

July 29 is the feast day of Saint Martha, who, in folklore tradition, is inseparable from the legendary Tarasque, which Louis Dumont has studied thoroughly.[3] There can be no doubt that this saint, like many other figures of *The Golden Legend,* is superimposed on old beliefs of Celtic paganism. Saint Martha supposedly came to Provence to preach the gospel, and simply by displaying the cross overcame a terrible dragon that had been devastating the region.

> At that time toward the west, on the banks of the Rhône next to a large rock in a wood between Arles and Avignon, there was an enormous dragon, half beast and half fish, which had killed many of those seeking to travel by and cross the river there, including horses and donkeys, and overturned the boats that sailed past on the Rhône. A number of armed knights made futile attempts to combat the creature, but the beast proved impossible to kill, for it would simply desert the wood and conceal itself in the river. Fat-

ter than a bull, longer than a horse, it had the face and head of a lion, teeth sharp as swords, the mane of a horse, a back that was as sharp as a hatchet, scales that were bristly and as cutting as an auger, six paws with bear claws, a serpent's tail, and a double shell like a tortoise on each side. Twelve bears or lions could not hold out against it. The local inhabitants, being absolutely incapable of killing it and having heard the praise of the miracles and exorcisms performed by the blessed Martha, went to her to implore that she drive this dragon from their land. The holy friend of God, the hostess of Christ, trusting in the power of the Divine Host, went there and found the dragon in the wood; it had captured someone and was eating him. She cast holy water upon it that she had brought and showed it a wooden cross. The defeated dragon became like a lamb; she bound it with her belt and the people tore it to pieces on the spot with spears and stones. Now the name of the dragon was Tirascurus, hence the wood took on the name Tirasconus [Tarascon], whereas formerly it had been named Nerluc, meaning "black wood," for the dark forests that were found there.

The battle against one or several demonic adversaries (the monsters of fire and flame) lie at the heart of the canicular myth. By exterminating the Tarasque, Martha civilizes an entire land that had been abandoned to the chaos created by a devastating monster and imposes divine law over paganism. The figure of the Tarasque is intriguing for its composite nature. In fact, this monster embodies the hybrid characteristic of creatures in Celtic and, more broadly, Indo-European mythology. The flying bear mentioned in the French Arthurian romance and the snake-fish-bird (otherwise known as the anguipede) of Gallo-Roman statuary, the multiple dragons of the Rogations who are winged, horned, and serpentlike in form all significantly echo the same mythic and gigantic creature that was called Gargan or gargoyle during the Middle Ages. The number of ioconographic representations (in Romanesque statuary, for example) cannot make us forget the simultaneously universal and unvarying nature of the Celtic monster.

July 22, Saint Magdalene's Day and the Canicule

In medieval hagiographic tradition, three female figures are associated with the canicule. The most important of them is Mary Magdalene, whose feast day is July 22. To understand this liaison between the canicular season and Saint Mary Magdalene, we must turn to the folklore and legends concerning this saint. For example, a legend from Upper Provence permits the discovery of several major motifs combined:

> Some miles away from Prads (in the Alps of Upper Provence) there was a small lake by the hamlet of Eaux-Chaudes [Hot Waters], a village that is deserted today. The patron saint of this place was Saint Magdalene. It was told how once, a long time ago, on Saint Magdalene's Day, a man of the hamlet and his wife had gone to harvest crops instead of taking part as they should in the services honoring the saint. They had brought their baby with them in a cradle and deposited it on the edge of the field, and while their baby slept, started harvesting. As punishment for this sacrilegious labor, the field collapsed and in its place an abyss was created that filled with water. The father, mother, and baby all drowned, and when the folk of the hamlet arrived on the scene, instead of a field they found the lake, *lou laus des Aigos Chaudos*. Only the cradle was floating on the water's surface.[4]

It is tempting to interpret this story as merely a pious invention of a clergy desperately seeking ways to incite devotion. But in so doing, we overlook two essential facts: through the centuries folklore (the oral tradition of tales and legends) has preserved traces of the old beliefs into which the Church inserted its own morality, and the biblical figure of Mary Magdalene (like other saints who succeeded other gods and goddesses, even the same deities) made it possible to adopt a pagan deity whom we are no longer capable of identifying clearly but whose existence must in some way be associated with the extraordinary popular devotion to Christianity's black Madonnas.

The Provençal legend quoted above is of interest in that it provides a precise date (Saint Magdalene's Day) for two seemingly independent occurrences: the appearance of a lake filled with hot water and the drowning of a small child (with his parents) in the water of this lake. The mention of a specific calendar date in a legend is actually quite rare. The particular date mentioned here reveals the adherence of these two seemingly independent occurrences to a major ritual date. We can connect the emergence of the two motifs to the "mythic" date that serves them as common reference. In other words, with this Provençal story, we are in the presence of the possible emergence of a festival or seasonal myth from a legend. The two motifs of the hot-water lake and the deaths of people for violating a taboo could be easily explained by the appearance of a third person (a sacred or fairylike figure) whom the legend intentionally leaves in the shadows and who finds a kind of Christian counterpart in Mary Magdalene.

It is evident that several layers are condensed in the Provençal legend of the lake of hot waters. On the first level, conforming to many toponymic narratives, the original legend describes the formation of an aquatic site, in this instance the lake of hot waters (*lou laus aigos chaudos*), which appears during the heart of the dog days. It is the conjunction of this period of time with a water-related phenomenon that inspires us to turn to mythological tradition for an explanation, not least because the dryness of the dog days is more often associated with drought than with an abundance of water.

As suggested by Mircea Eliade, a myth of a great flood, whether cyclical or characteristic of the end of the world, can be found at the root of the episode.[5] The annual flood of the Nile during the canicular period, marking the beginning of a new season, was the subject of both a theological and a mythological interpretation. Any deluge was associated with a ritual sin that brought about the anger of a divine creature.* In the legend of the lake of hot waters, it is Mary Magdalene who assumes the role of demiurge.

---

*[While the flooding of the Nile was not associated with sin as we define the term *sin* today, the god Sin, who gave his name to the idea of transgression, was involved with the annual Nile flood. —*Trans.*]

It is common to find similar episodes in Indo-European mythology: Georges Dumézil studied the motif of the sudden overflowing of a lake or the rapid appearance of a stagnant body of water that becomes a deep lake and found in the work of Dionysius of Halicarnassus a Roman myth concerning the overflowing of a lake during the dog days:[6]

> When the Romans were besieging the Veientes about the time of the rising of the dog star, the season when lakes and all rivers are most apt to fail, with the single exception of the Egyptian Nile, a certain lake not less than one hundred and twenty stades from Rome, in the Alban mountains . . . at a time when neither rains nor snowstorms had occurred nor any other cause perceptible to human beings, received such an increase to its waters that it inundated a large part of the region lying round the mountains.

A similar story can be found in other Indo-European mythologies, particularly in Celtic and Iranian legends. All these narratives are connected by calendrical and onamastic analogies, pointing to variations on a theme typical of Indo-European tradition. The Provençal legend can be classified among the variants based on the Roman Neptunalia (celebrated on July 23).

The second level of the Provençal legend is formed by a layer of Christianization. According to Christian belief, the refusal to attend important holy services could not go unpunished. Similar legends of retribution exist for other important liturgical dates. In all of these the miscreants are punished by heaven for deliberately transgressing in their obligation to attend Christmas Mass, Easter Mass, or that of another holiday. For example, the legend of the cursed dancers records that young people who intentionally neglected their religious duties on the day of a high feast were punished by being swallowed up by a lake or the earth itself.[7] The thirteenth-century *Miracles of Notre Dame of Chartres* corroborates the ancient nature of this motif: Miracles 2, 25, and 26 address the punishment of certain individuals who have worked on a day—the feast of Saint Agatha (February 4), Candlemas (February 2), or the feast of Saint Germain of Auxerre (July 31)—during which labor was proscribed. All of these texts preserve very ancient local traditions that remained vital until the late Middle Ages through an oral culture that periodically reformulated pre-Christian heritage.[8]

Thus this motif of heavenly retribution appears in much folklore. In fact, Paul Sebillot gathered together several legends in which "the non-observance of holy days provoked divine vengeance"—specifically non-observance of the feast of Mary Magdalene, which we have seen in the Provençal legend:

> Because the inhabitants of a village between Barjols and Brignoles had made a mockery of the feast day of Saint Magdalene, a storm broke out, the streams swelled, and water even poured out of the earth to swallow up the sacrilegious town and in its place is the pond of Bras. Every year, during the night preceding Saint Magdalene's Day, the sorrowful cries of the wretches who were drowned there and who are condemned to eternal damnation can be distinctly heard.[9]

Here we find the same mythological ingredients that appear in the Provençal tale. The story of the mysterious appearance of the waters of the canicule (swollen rivers, water gushing out of the ground) originally contained no reference to Magdalene, but when this region was converted to Christianity, Mary Magdalene could occupy the profane terrain of this aquatic magic and thus the sudden appearance of raging water was diverted to the benefit of her cult. Henri Dontenville has quite rightly reminded us that the topynomic use of Magdalene's name is intended to conceal the traces of ancient deities connected to the Celtic worship of water, stones, or woods:

> Starting in 1200, her name began to pop up almost everywhere; it was consigned to dolmens, caves, and mountains where we can still detect the traces of ancient beliefs. One of the pilgrimage routes of Gallic and pre-Gallic times, leading from the Carnute forest

to Mont-Saint-Michel, is marked on the edge of woods by places named after Magdalene . . . In Finistère, Mary Magdalene threw at the devil the stones she was carrying in her apron, and this is how people there explain the aligned stones of Lestriniou.[10]

In other legends it is the fairy Melusine herself who inspires the existence of certain megaliths. Interestingly, in popular mythology, at least, Magdalene and Melusine are interchangeable.

Another Provençal Magdalene legend associates an inundation with a transgression regarding the worship of the saint (or the pagan figure from which she descended) on Saint Magdalene's Day: Mary Magdalene was particularly irritated at the sight of people working and blaspheming on her feast day, July 22, and therefore caused horses, carts, and the impious to be swallowed up in the *iero aprefundado,* a water-filled hole 180 feet in circumference and 75 feet deep, located within the confines of Nans-les-Pins, which sits between Jaudard and Le Bori.

The existence of pagan rites near aquatic sites is historically proved by an eighth-century sermon that hurls this anathema: "Whoever on the occasion of the Neptunalia (July 23) prays near the sea or even a river that flows out of a cape, may he know that he will be stripped of both faith and baptism."[11] The name Neptune is related to that of an autoch-

Fig. 8.1. Saint Mary Magdalene

thonous deity who has left numerous traces in medieval folklore and literature: the *neton* or *nuiton,* which belongs to the category of fairy beings who haunt rivers, lakes, and springs.[12]

Under these conditions, it becomes obvious that the figure and worship of Mary Magdalene were intended to conceal an old pagan figure (fairy or *nuiton* in the Middle Ages, mother goddess for Celtic paganism). The Provençal legend of the Saint Marys of the Sea allows us to confirm this.

The Three Marys and the Three Fairies

It is fairly common knowledge that Provence's conversion to Christianity is rooted in the pious legend of the Saint Marys of the Sea, three eminent figures who are alleged to have landed on the Provençal coast to escape the persecutions of Christ's disciples. From our viewpoint, this legend appears quite like a myth—that is, it seems both a fabulous story intended to induce belief and a foundational tale that reflects pre-Christian beliefs.

Who were these Saint Marys of the Sea? The first was Mary Jacobus, mother of James the Lesser and sister of the Virgin Mary; the second was Mary Salome, mother of the apostles James and John; and the third was Mary of Magdala, better know as Mary Magdalene. Traditionally they have in their company a humble servant and companion named Sarah, who became the legendary patron of the Gypsies in the Camargue region. Even today they pay her special devotion in the crypt of the Church of Our Lady of the Sea. Also accompanying these three Marys were Maximin, the resurrected Lazarus, and his sister Martha. This entire band arrived in Provence around the year 40, after fleeing the persecution of the disciples of Christ, and subsequently dispersed in order to spread the gospel in Provence. According to tradition, Maximin went to Aix, Lazarus to Marseilles, Martha to Tarascon, and Mary Magdalene to Sainte-Baume. The other two Marys and their servant, Sarah, remained alone on the beach where they had made landfall. Archaeological excavations conducted around 1446 by the chamberlain of King René unearthed the alleged relics of the Saint Marys of the Sea in a chapel located in the center of the currently existing church dedicated to them.[13]

The tradition of the Marys is presented as a beautifully poetic legend that has seems to be quite a tall tale with no historical basis. There is no point, however, in debating the validity of the foundations of this tradition. Rather, we need to ask ourselves why such a legend exists, why it was able to develop at this site, and why it has inspired such a lasting Christian myth.

The oldest traces of a cult dedicated to the three Marys goes back to the eleventh century, to a *Life of Saint Magdalene,* in a manuscript by Saint-Arnoul of Crépy. Corroborating this date, use of the proper name Martha began to spread only during the eleventh century, an essential clue to the rapid historic development of the cult of Saint Martha.[14] Still, we must examine closely the site on which grew the legend of the three Saint Marys of the Sea.

The engineer Charles Lenthéric, who has studied southern sites known for their abundance of legends, carefully inspected the one associated with the three Marys:

> The two bas-reliefs next to the Bauz, extremely crude and carved in the rock and whose ancient origin is incontestable, are called the Trémaïe and the Gaïe. They are located about 800 feet apart from each other and about 100 feet below the village. The Trémaïe (*three imagined Marys?*) represent three upright figures on foot, draped in long robes; they are quite mutilated but are also fairly handsome. The Gaïe or Caïe are much less well-preserved; it is hard to distinguish in them two human shapes from the waist up, also covered by large garments.[15]

An imaginative archaeologist believed he could discern in the Trémaïe the Roman general Marius, his wife Julia, and Martha the Syrian, who was a constant companion of the generalissimo. Such a hypothesis underestimates the pre-Christian mythic layer that exists at a particular site prior to the establishment of a hagiographic legend there. In fact, not just any saint can be established just anywhere. Almost throughout the whole of Gaul there are triads comparable to that of the Trémaïé. In fact, Gallo-Roman statuary preserves countless testimonies to triple Celtic mother goddesses, the three "mothers," often depicted side by side, to whom the Gauls dedicated a prominent worship.[16]

The three Marys, then, could be nothing other than the Christian metamorphosis of a triad of fairies. Bishop Burchard of Worms compared the medieval fairies to the Three Sisters and the Three Fates of antiquity. The *Jeu de la Feuillée* depicts the fairy Morgue (or Morgana) next to her two inseparable companions, Maglore and Arsile.[17] As has been clearly noted by A. Maury, "the number three reappeared in a crowd of legends related to these mysterious women. It is three fairies who built the Castle of Fairies three leagues from Tours; it is three pale, blonde fairies who brought to Langeac, in the Velay region, the megalithic monuments found there, and so forth.[18]

Sarah, the Black Madonna

The mythic figure of Sarah should herself be placed within the context of folkloric beliefs concerning fairies. Sarah the Black One is what folklore calls a Saracen, who, rather than being an Arab woman, is first and foremost a Cthonian, fairylike creature similar to those who haunt the traditional sites of the Otherworld: fountains, springs, forests, caves, and other underground places.

Mistral's *Mireille* (Chant 12) provides a perfect evocation of the cthonian site where the cult of Sarah is celebrated:

> Already, the great saints—she [Mireille] saw the blond church—in the far-of lapping sea—growing like a ship making for shore . . . In the top part of the church—are three altars, three chapels built one on top of the other in blocks of living stone—In the underground chapel—Saint Sarah is worshipped—by the brunette bohemians—the one that sits higher holds the altar to God.

On the pillars of the sanctuary—the narrow mortuary chapel —of the Maries lifts its vault into heaven—with its relics, sacred bequests from which grace flows like rain . . . Four keys seal the shrines—the cypress shrines with their tops.

Once every hundred years they are opened—Blessed, blessed when they are opened—is he who can see and touch them!—Good weather will have its bark, and good star—and the sprouts of his trees—will have baskets of fruit—and his believing soul will have good fortune eternally.

According to the testimony of Strabo (*Geographia,* Book 4), the people of Marseilles built a temple to Diana of Ephesus on the littoral of the Camargue. Could Sarah the Black One be a Diana of Ephesus imported from the East? This is hardly likely. The fact that she is worshiped in an underground chapel, just like the Black Madonna of the cathedral of Chartres, instead calls for a comparison to the Celtic legends of fairies finding a haven in caves and other wild places.

Starting in the tenth century, a Black Madonna, the Bouéno Méro Negro, was worshiped in the crypt of Saint Victor in Marseilles. During Candlemas, this blackened Madonna receives a parade of pilgrims carrying green wax candles. If carefully preserved throughout the year, these candles, it is said, will protect the home from lightning. The same kind of procession with ordinary candles takes place during the Feast of Assumption on August 15, in the very middle of the dog days, a time when it was again necessary to exorcise the threat of storms.

The Black Madonna of Montserrat in Spain or that of Rocamadour in the Lot region of France is the focus of a syncretic worship in which the pagan rite runs parallel to Christian practices. A true heiress of the fairies, the Black Madonna was earlier confused with the wild woman sometimes known as Sarassine.* As it happens, French folklore peddles quite a few legends about Saracens and Sarrasines; because they have allegedly left traces of their presence in places that were never reached

---

*[Sarassine is the feminine form of the French word for Saracen. —*Trans.*]

by the Arab invasions, we have to accept that they are mythical creatures rather than people from the East. On the level of the medieval imaginal realm, then, we must distinguish the Saracen in whom reappears the fantasy figures of fairies and revenants from the Muslim who reflects completely different historical realities. In fact, when the literary texts of the Middle Ages bring up Arab civilization, it is usually in the guise of a mythical and purely imaginary world, rather than representational of any historical or social truth. In this context, the Saracen (male and female) is first and foremost a being from the Otherworld who is marked by his or her inclusion in the dark world of ghosts. This being's survival in Christianity is testified to by Sarah and all the other Black Madonnas.

Christopher and the Dog

The July 25 feast day of the dog-headed Saint Christopher opens an important commemorative period in which we can find all the major aspects of the canicular myth of the Middle Ages. This Christianized figure of an old pre-Christian deity invites us to look carefully at his hagiographic tradition. We can note that his feast day is the same as that of Saint James of Compostela, who is honored by the famous pilgrimage through Galicia.

According to legend, the barbarian Reprobus (the "reprobate") is born in the land of Canaan during the third century C.E. in the form of

Fig. 8.2. Saint Christopher

a giant with a terrifying face resembling that of a dog. Reprobus, his Latin name, was undoubtedly formed from the Aramaic word *rabrab*, which means "giant." Because he wants to serve a master worthy of his strength, he first offers his services to King Philip of Lycia (which means "land of the wolves" in Greek), then to Satan himself, who terrifies the king. Given that Satan, in turn, is terrified by the cross, Reprobus quickly determines that it is Christ who will be his definitive master.

Eventually, a hermit persuades Reprobus to use his strength and great height to help travelers cross a river. One day, while he bears a child on his shoulders, the water begins to rise. The little boy becomes as heavy as lead, but with superhuman effort, Reprobus manages to reach the other shore. The child then declares to him: "Not only have you carried the world, but also the one who created it. I am the king whom you have been seeking and whom you unknnowingly have been serving. Henceforth, you will no longer be called Reprobus, but Christopher, 'he who has carried Christ.' Now, plant your staff into the ground." Christopher obeyed and his staff grew covered with leaves and dates.

So goes the legend. But what is the origin of Saint Christopher's dog's head? Pierre Saintyves looked to Egypt and the Egyptian dog-god Anubis as the logical mythical ancestor of Christopher. Yet as the tradition of cynocephalic deities proves, the dog's head is a feature that undoubtedly belongs to a long series of gods.[19]

Beneath the giant Christopher we find a boatman or ferryman psychopomp comparable to Orion in Greek mythology. In fact, this figure, especially as represented by the figure of the dog, goes back to myths of the descent into hell. The dog is also associated with the Beyond in Celtic folklore. In Brittany it is believed that a black dog, Yeun Ellez, will meet those on the road through the swamps of hell. Moreover, meeting this dog is an omen predicting an imminent tempest or catastrophe, and it is most often considered one of the aspects of the devil who seeks his prey among sinners. This dog figure is commingled with the club-wielding giant of the Mesnie Hellequin, who leads the Wild Hunt. In his mythical persona, then, Saint Christopher combines both the giant and the dog of this hunt.

One proof that the dog is seen in the Celtic imgination as a possible intermediary between this world and the Otherworld is the worship devoted to the holy greyhound Guignefort in the region of Châtillon-sur-Chalaronne. Basing his work on the testimony of Etienne de Bourbon, Jean-Claude Schmitt showed that the worship of Saint Guignefort was situated at the heart of an entirely pagan belief that Christianity attempted to eradicate.

> Women with sick children would carry their offspring to the supposed site of the sepulchre of a sacred dog. They followed a custom of offering it salt and other things. On the bushes that surrounded the site they would hang the swaddling clothes of the ill child and stick nails in the trees that grew in this spot. They would then pass the naked child between the adjacent trunks of two trees, imploring the fauns to take this child, who they said was in their care, and return him fat and safe and sound.[20]

A certain legend lends legitimacy to this rite. It tells that one day, a dog saved a child from being bitten by a snake. Because the dog's muzzle was splattered with blood after his battle with the snake, the child's parents believed that the dog had devoured their infant. They quickly slew the animal, but immediately after, upon seeing their child safe and sound, they regretted their action. The dog's body was cast into a well located in front of the gate to the castle, and the cult of the greyhound was born at this specific location.

In the thirteenth century, the inquisitor Etienne de Bourbon visited Châtillon-sur-Chalaronne and learned of the rites and traditions surrounding the greyhound. Horrified, he decided to put an end to these practices. He convoked a gathering of all the area's inhabitants, ordered the trees cut down, and exhumed the bones of the dog, which he then had burned in a bonfire. Finally, he proclaimed a prohibition on the "barbaric" cult. Yet it was to no avail; the worship continued as strong as ever, although in the meantime the dog was canonized in the form of Saint Guignefort, whose memory became commingled with that of the greyhound. Thus the worship of Saint Guignefort offers yet another example of the Christianizing of mythology in the Middle Ages.

Upon discovering that it could not eliminate the beliefs and rites of paganism, the Church hastened to transform them to conform to its teachings. To the Church, this transfer of sacrality was a means of guiding toward Christianity a miscreant populace that would find new reasons to honor its old gods while benefiting from divine favors that, until then, had been denied them. By assuming the old superstitions or by at least adapting these beliefs to the spirit of evangelical revelation, the Church spoke a language that the uneducated masses could understand. To Church hierarchy, this was the price that had to be paid to convert the pagans. All that survives today in what is sometimes called the folk religion harks back to this cultural compromise, which allowed the entry of certain forms of paganism into the ritual and sacred framework of Christianity. The period of the dog days offers particularly suggestive examples of this pagan mythology gone astray. Mary Magdalene, Christopher, Martha, and Guignefort offer examples of the same dialogue between Christianity and the archaic, pagan memory of the West.

NINE

Saint Michael on Mount Gargan

The vestiges of Carnival are quite evident on Saint Michael's Day, September 29, though the essential features of the mythology and ritual surrounding this period have become blurred over the course of the centuries. Ancient testimonies, however, make it plausible that this date was the occasion of ritual manifestations equal in importance to those that took place at other times of the year.

Today, Saint Michael's Day no longer offers us an opportunity to celebrate as we do during Carnival. Yet as late as the eighteenth century a priest mentions a New Year's Eve–like celebration on the night of September 29.[1] In the Germanic world, libations were always planned for this day, and in Russia, Michael is the name of the bear that is emblematic of that country. Of course, the archetypal figure of this Carnival animal does not by chance prowl around this date. As Claude Gaignebet has emphasized, the rhythm of the forty days is associated with the emergence of bears (or the Wild Man) in the folklore calendar, and Saint Michael's Day is plainly placed on this ursine axis of the seasons.

Saint Michael of Peril

All the pagan mythology concerning the autumn equinox is centered on a symbolic site: Mont-Saint-Michel, the pagan memory of which remains visible beneath its Christian patina. And Michael remains

Fig. 9.1. Saint Michael

closely associated with this major site of the West on which countless Christians converge. Because of this fact, the famous Norman mountain constituted a mythological Mecca of the Middle Ages, during which it had been given the name Saint Michael of the Peril.

In *The Golden Legend,* Jacobus de Voragine tells the fundamental story that earned the mount its status as a sacred Christian site:

> The holy solemnity of S. Michael is said, appearing, dedication, victory, and memory. The apparition of this angel is manifold. The first is when he appeared on the Mount of Gargan. This mountain is in Naples, which is named Gargan and is by the city named Syponte. And in the year of our Lord three hundred and ninety, was in the same city of Syponte a man who was named Garganus, which, after some books, had taken that name of the mountain, or else the mountain took the name of the man. And he was right rich and had a great multitude of sheep and beasts, and as they pastured about the sides of the mountains, it happed that a bull left the other beasts and went upon high on the mountain and returned not home again with the other beasts. Then this rich

man, the owner, took a great multitude of servants and did seek this bull all about, and at the last he was found on high on the mountain, by the entry of a hole or a cave. And then the master was wroth because he had strayed alone from other beasts, and he made one of his servants to shoot an arrow at him. And anon the arrow returned with the wind and smote him that had shot it, wherewith they of the city were troubled with this thing, and went to the bishop and inquired of him what was to be done on this thing that was so wonderful. And then he commanded them to fast three days and to pray unto God. And when this was done, S. Michael appeared to the bishop, saying: Know ye that this man is so hurt by my will. I am Michael the archangel, which will that this place be worshipped on earth, and will have it surely kept. And therefore I have proved that I am keeper of this place by the demonstrance and showing of this thing.

This fundamental text contains three major elements that profane belief introduced into the heart of the medieval Christian mythology of the saint: the discovery of a sacred site by an animal, the arrow that turns back against the one who shot it, and the name of Saint Michael's bull, Gargan.

The Sacred Bull

The legend of the bull, discoverer of Mount of Gargan, now known as Mont-Saint-Michel, is indeed an ancient tale. The *Homilies* of the Venerable Bede (672–735)[2] provide the earliest record of this legend, and Flodoard (894–966) places it in the middle of the tenth century.[3] This Christian myth is based on the watering down of a pagan myth concerning the sacred bull. In the Montoise legend, the bull that leads men to the sacred site is performing the role of Hermes. He guides humans to the archangel Michael, who in turn can guide souls to the holy light: "May Saint Michael, the standard bearer lead them into the holy light" (*sed signifer sanctus Michael repraesentet eas in lucen sanctum*), as it is stated in the prayer of the Mass for the Dead. Pierre Saintyves clearly grasped that Saint Michael "succeeded" the ancient Hermes or the Roman Mercury. As if emphasizing this mythical line of descent, the toponym Saint-Michel-Mont-Mercure in the Vendée (between Nantes and la Rochelle) combines in succession the names of the two psychopomp deities honored at the same site.

The name Gargan obviously brings to mind the name of the giant Gargantua—and it so happens that the mythical association of a giant with certain mountains is well established in the oldest medieval literature, which demonstrates its connection to an earlier mythical tradition. In Béroul's *Romance of Tristan,* a solitary hermit named Ogrin dwells in the Morrois Forest. To allow Isolde to return to King Mark after her flight from his court, he plays the role of go-between. Ogrin goes to the mountain (here Saint Michael's Mount in Cornwall) to buy luxuriant clothing that he then offers to the queen. Though the book does not tell us where Ogrin gets the money to purchase such sumptuous outfits, the answer can be found in the myth of giants that Béroul uses as part of the basis for his tale. It is obvious that Ogrin, a barely disguised representation of the Wild Man, appears here as an avatar of the ogre, who, as can be seen in countless folktales, always possesses immense treasures. As implied because of his relationship to ogres, Ogrin knows this mythical wealth is stored on a mountain, to be used whenever he needs it. Based on the testimony provided by the *Romance of Tristan,* Saint Michael's Mount is clearly Orgin's Mountain—the Ogre's Mountain.[4] The Anglo-Norman saga recalls the existence of this ogrelike figure who haunts the mountain, and King Arthur confronts and kills there a terrible giant who had been a thief and rapist of women.[5]

The myth relating to the "Christian" birth of Mont-Saint-Michel is not isolated. For instance, almost everywhere in France and throughout the rest of Europe, local legends recount the accidental discovery of a statue of the Virgin by a bovine or similar animal. A Christian site then comes to supplant what was once a pagan site. The *Histoire illustrée des pèlerinages français de la très sainte Vierge Marie* (An Illustrated

History of French Pilgrimages for the Holy Virgin Mary),[6] published in 1890 by the Reverend Father Drochon, is a beautiful anthology of pagan myths that have been Christianized in the interest of Marian devotion. In reality, this naive work presents to those who know how to read it a marvelous collection of pagan myths that are barely covered by a Christian veneer.

The pilgrimage in honor of Our Lady of Font Romean in Odeillo, for example, has its origin in a pious bull legend. The site's sacredness is connected to a spring (Font-Romeu means "the fountain of the Roman pilgrim") located behind the current high altar beneath the niche that holds the Virgin's statue. The figure, it is said, was miraculously discovered at the beginning of the twelfth century by a bull that had pawed at the ground with its hoof and its horns.

A statue of Our Lady of Romigier in Manosque was discovered under similar circumstances: Two steers pulling a plow came to a halt in front of a thornbush and refused to go any farther. The plowman was stunned at their obstinacy and called on several neighbors for assistance. Upon digging the ground at this site, they spotted a statue of the Virgin in a white marble sarcophagus. The statue, called Our Lady of Romigier, has been worshipped ever since. The word *romigier* comes from the Provençal *roumi,* meaning "bush," and calls to mind the sacred values that the ancient Celts assigned to trees and bushes.

In all these tales, the bull plays the role of a fairy animal initiated into the secrets of the tutelary deities of the site. He is undoubtedly the metamorphosis of a god, the pagan and divine ogre whose magical powers he appears to incorporate.

Also belonging to Celtic tradition is the second significant motif of the legend, that of the arrow shot at an animal that mysteriously turns from its target to head toward the archer. The Montoise legend is not its sole appearance in medieval literature of Celtic origin. A twelfth-century lay by Marie de France tells how Guigemar, a renowned hunter, shoots an arrow at a white doe in the bushes. After it touches the animal, the arrow, as if enchanted, turns back to the person who shot it.

Certainly, other examples of this hunter theme can found in

mythological tradition; we need only recall the story of Acteon.* Yet the Celtic "version" of the Montoise legend and the lay written by Marie de France are significant in their suggestions. If an arrow can be turned back upon the one who shot it, it is because the animal targeted is the incarnation of a deity who possesses characteristics that the Middle Ages defined as magical. In other words, the bull of Mont-Saint-Michel is no ordinary animal; it is a divine bull, an animal fairy that can be compared to the mysterious bulls of Celtic origin that have been discovered by chance or unearthed in archaeological digs. In Avrigney, a bronze statue of a three-horned bull dating from Gallo-Roman times was discovered in just this way in 1756. It alone demonstrates the importance of the bull among the divine figures of the Celtic religion, an importance that speaks to a heritage going back to the sacred cows of Hinduism.

For too long now the specific features of Celtic myths have gone unrecognized in the shadow of the better-known and more prestigious Greek myths. When they have been recognized, people have endeavored to make Celtic myths pale imitations of the legends of the Greeks. In fact, the affinity of the Celtic myths and those of the Greek or Germanic world can be best explained by their common Indo-European heritage.

Gargan

In the legend of Mont-Saint-Michel, the herdsman of the sacred mountain goes by the name Gargan, who obviously foreshadows the large Rabelaisian figure, who was himself preceded by the mythical giant celebrated in the Gargantuan chronicles. Yet we can specifically find twelfth-century corroboration of the name Gargan in the romance *Florimont,* written in 1118 by Aymon de Varennes. In this tale the author, a native of the Lyonnaise region, gives a detailed description of a giant named Garganeüs that can leave no doubt concerning his mythic origins:

---

*[Acteon is the name of the hunter who happened to see the goddess Diana bathing naked and, as punishment, was torn to pieces by his own dogs. —*Trans.*]

Garganeüs . . . Had the head of a leopard
That cast an evil look
And the body of a flying guivre. *
Never was living man so huge
Starting at the region of his thighs
Was the Snake and the Fish

FLORIMONT, A. HILKA EDITION, VERSES 1973–78

This giant has a leopard's head that casts a deadly gaze and the body of the guivre (or vouivre), a flying giant. Starting from the thighs, he is described as a snake or a fish—a description that allows us to join Garganeüs and Melusine in the same archetype that transcends their apparent sexual opposition.

Gallo-Roman archaeology enables us to locate the prototype for all these figures, for Garganeüs possesses the same fishlike aspect as the anguipede of Gallo-Roman columns, which can also be found in numerous examples of ancient statuary.[7] For an example, we can look to the third-century Gallo-Roman column discovered in Merten in 1878 and now on display at the Metz Museum. This find is testimony to the syncretism of Celtic and Roman beliefs at a time when the Celts (Gauls) were finally erecting effigies of their gods.

The interpretation of such a monument is obviously complex, for it appeals to several levels of meaning that are not always easy to disentangle. The depiction on this column of a Jupiterian rider wearing the garb of the triumphant Roman emperor might illustrate the *pax romana* and might also suggest the political supremacy of the Roman god (and consequently the Roman religion) over the Gallic anguipede deity, with its body that ends in a fish tail. In fact, this Gallic god is shown tangled beneath the god-emperor's horse in the posture of the defeated. We might therefore deduce that in this Roman interpretation of a Gallic god and religious theme, the two deities (the Roman Jupiter and the Gallic anguipede) possess the same mythical attributes of celestial sovereignty,

---

*[The guivre is a mythical beast similar to a dragon and a basilisk. —*Trans.*]

although Jupiter has dethroned his dark rival. Yet the same cavalier can also bring to mind the theme of the infernal ride or Mesnie Hellequin that features a ghost rider dashing through the air with his army of shades.

We can also note the protean nature of the monster in this monument. The Lorraine museum of Nancy owns a similar Gallo-Roman statue in which the anguipede appears with clearly visible wings. In this depiction it has become a bird and is reminiscent of some of the flying monsters that appear in the Arthurian legends and in the folklore of the Rogations (the duck-beaked dragon of Metz, for example). The anguipede (the fish-man or snake-man) directly brings to mind the well-known Melusine representations of Romanesque statuary and the iconography of illuminated manuscripts. This half-human, half-animal fairy is none other than an avatar of the giant, the master of the Otherworld and a major figure in the Celtic pantheon. He simultaneously possesses gigantic versions of typical human features and features borrowed from birds, snakes, and fish. This concentration of features from the different aspects of the animal kingdom is what gives this figure his true divine nature.

The names Gargantua and Garganeüs are obviously comparable. It might be helpful at this point to look more closely at this affinity of names, for a myth is transmitted primarily by names, whether proper ones or toponyms. Henri Dontenville and his disciples have listed all the place-names containing Gargan. As examples, we can point to Livry-Gargan (Seine-Saint-Denis), Garganvillar (Tarn-et-Garonne), and Gargas (Haute-Garonne-et-Vaucluse), along with the numerous Mount Gargans. We can also cite Gargenville, Garges-lès-Gonesse, Gargilesse Dampierre, and countless other place-names. A good number of these toponyms existed long before the time of Rabelais. Gargas in fact takes us all the way back to Neolithic times via the many caves that exist in this area. The existence of a mythical figure associated with the name Gargan was inscribed on this Norman high ground long before the sixteenth century and prompts the mythologist or historian of religions not to underestimate the certain mythological continuity between the ancient Celtic world and the Christian universe of the Middle Ages.

The Dog Lady and October 9, Saint Denis's Day

The legend of Saint Denis, who is commemorated on October 9, contains a number of mythological elements that go far toward helping us to understand the pagan roots of medieval mythology. This legend, developed in several stages, allows us to follow its growth. In the sixth century, Gregory of Tours was the first to mention the decapitation of Saint Denis. In the seventh century, an anonymous writer, who declared his version was based on an oral tradition, added a detail to the decapitation: After having been parted from the martyr's body, the head continued to move and give praise to God. In the ninth century, the legend was completed by the merger of two figures who were undoubtedly independent of each other before this time.

Born to a wealthy Athenian family nine years after the death of Jesus Christ, gifted in mathematics and astrology, Dionysius (known as Denis) became more learned in the latter science before becoming a magistrate (archon) of Athens. He was converted to Christianity by Saint Paul and left his home to preach the gospel in Europe, arriving in Paris to set up numerous places of worship.

Arrested by the Roman governor Fescennius, he was subjected

Fig. 9.2. Saint Denis

to several forms of martyrdom. While his head was held imprisoned by a stone, his limbs were mutilated with a whip until his bones were exposed, whereupon he was given a bath in his own blood, yet he still refused to renounce his faith. Stretched out over a white-hot grill, he ignored his burns. The lions to whom he had been thrown as food came and licked his feet. Placed in an oven, he emerged heartier than when he entered. Even when crucified, his faith remained unshakable. Finally, the Roman governor ordered him to be decapitated on a Parisian hill dedicated to Mercury that was subsequently known as the mountain of martyrs (Montmartre). Once he had been decapitated, however, Saint Denis stood up, retrieved his head with his hands, and carried it north of Paris to the site of a town that has been known by his name ever since.

This pretty legend has every appearance of a pious invention intended to shroud the relics of a tenacious pagan myth that preceded Christianity. Indeed, the cellar of the Basilica of Saint Denis has yielded remnants of pagan worship that are much older than the founding of the monument. Could this worship have been centered on a sacred head that would later be turned into the head of Saint Denis?

Certainly, there is no shortage of Celtic examples of magical decapitations. The Irish mythological texts that constitute the best conservatory of the Celtic tradition in this regard offer the example of *The Feast of Bricriu*,[8] during which there takes place a decapitation similar to that of Saint Denis. Just as in the legend of Saint Denis, instead of dying, the decapitated individual picks up his head and leaves. In her book entitled *Dieux et Héros celtes,* Marie-Louise Sjoestedt summarizes this important text, which is itself the adaptation of an older Celtic myth in which the rite of the severed head is invested with a sacred value: The giant Curoi, seeking to challenge the heroes of Ulster, shows up in the middle of a feast holding a chopping block in one hand and an ax in the other. He asks that a courageous hero cut off his head and agree to have his own head lopped off the following day. When a hero accepts the challenge, Curoi lends him the ax and places his head on the chopping block. The Irish hero cuts off the head of the giant, who immediately stands up, picks up his head, his chopping block, and his ax and, holding his head to his chest, submerges himself in the nearby lake that is his home. Indeed, the theme of the severed head plays an essential role in the whole Celtic religion.[9]

Likewise, several medieval romances featuring the knights of King Arthur display this same motif: the thirteenth-century romance *Humbaut* and the English *Sir Gawain and the Green Knight*. What is more, the motif of the severed head occupies a choice position in the Grail romances. In fact, in a Welsh version of the story of the Grail it is explicitly stated that the Grail contains a severed head, a sinister detail that Chrétien de Troyes took pains to erase from his famous *Conte du Graal,* written around 1183.

Saint Denis is therefore connected to a long mythic tradition that combines decapitation with rites of founding and fertility. Perhaps this is why Saint Denis, whose name etymologically derives from Dionysus, the god of the vine and wine, is celebrated during the time of the grape harvests. We can note that Saint Denis's two companions, Saint Rusticus and Saint Eleutherius, bear the nicknames traditionally given in antiquity to the god Dionysus.

The current town of Saint-Denis was originally called Catulacum or Catuliacum. We can easily discover the origin of this name by taking into consideration the Celtic myth covered by the Christianized legend of Saint Denis. The *Gesta Dagoberti* relates that a Lady Catula recieved the severed head of Saint Denis and took great care of it.[10] Now, Catula means "bitch" in Latin and thereby echoes the myth of the bird-dog of the Mesnie Hennequin and is obviously reminiscent of the dog that travels in the boat of Saint Tropez, who was also decapitated. Additionally, we can note the presence of the helpful women in other legends concerning the decapitated. In the legend of Saint Andeol, for example, a woman named Tullie picks up the sacred head of the martyr. Interestingly, Tullie appears to be a contracted and Romanized form of Catula, the dog-lady of Celtic myth.

Saint Denis possesses numerous doubles almost everywhere in France. The image of the cephalophoric saint (referring to one who carries his head after it has been cut off) is common in medieval hagiography. Pierre

Saintyves has detected more than one hundred male and female cephalophoric saints whose worship is spread everywhere throughout Europe. In truth, these are simply the reproductions of the same myth and rite of decapitation reflecting the archetypal figure of the giant and the Christianized form of an old pagan fertility rite.

Saint Bruno, the Bear of the Mountains

As we have seen, the mythic figure of the bear is ubiquitous in Christian mythology. There are countless numbers of saints known by a name based on the French or Latin words for bear—Saint Ours, Saint Ursin, and so forth—as well as names based on other similar etymological associations (such as Saint Bernard—from *bär,* a Germanic source, and *–art,* the Celtic name for this animal). But what relationship with the bear is maintained by good Saint Bruno, founder of the Chartreuse order north of Grenoble? We should first note that Bruno means "the brown one," which immediately brings to mind the use of hair color as a distinguishing characteristic. The brown one, however, can also be understood as the hirsute one—that is, someone covered with brown hair—which immediately leads to the figure of the brown bear, an animal designated by an entire series of similar phrases, as folklorist Claude Gaignebet reminds us: the hairy one, the uncle, the Wild Man, the furry man, the plantigrade, the swollen foot, the licker, the honeyed one, the old man of the mountain, the master of the forest, and so on.[11] Indeed, Brun is the very name given the bear in the *Roman de Renart.* Of course, however, we must view this etymological explanation for the name in light of a hagiographic episode recorded in the *Life of Saint Hughes, Bishop of Grenoble.*[12]

The story recounts that Bruno and six of his companions were looking for land on which to build a monastery and were drawn to Grenoble by the saintly reputation of Bishop Hughes. As it turned out, the bishop had a dream that convinced him to satisfy Bruno's request: He saw God himself building a dwelling for his glory on a mountain in the wilderness and also saw seven stars indicating the location of this building. Now, Bruno and his companions numbered seven, the same number as the stars in the bishop's dream. Furthermore, these stars in the dream indicated the destination of the dwelling was north, and the massif of Chartreuse, where the monastery was constructed, is located to the north of Grenoble. Astronomically, Bruno and his six companions symbolized the stars in the Big Dipper,* with Bruno being more distinctive than the others by the ursine symbolism of his name. Indeed, once they had settled in Chartreuse, the monks lived like bears in their wild surroundings.

The Giant Gug in *The Prophecies of Merlin*

An essential part of the myths concerning giants in the West is centered on Mount Gargan (Mont-Saint-Michel). Yet while the association of Gargan with a specific mountain is irrefutable, this does not exhaust the primordial and wide-reaching aspects of the myth of the giant. There is a well-known Mount Gargan near Rouen, for example. A locality by the same name with the reputation of being haunted is found in Houdivilliers, in the Beauvais arrondisement.[13] Henri Dontenville has listed all these gargantuan sites but some doubt the age of the mythic traditions connected to them. Here it is helpful to turn to the calendar. If Gargan(tua) is truly a name that is emblematic of the key figure of Carnival, the myth of the giant should reveal a temporal component that will shed light on this association of Carnival time and the Gargantuan myth.

Looking at a short extract from *The Prophecies of Merlin,* a French text from the end of the thirteenth century,[14] can allow us to grasp the connection between Carnival and the figure of the giant. Here we can find in its embryonic state a legendary tradition concerning a giant whose malefic power haunted an entire region. The appearance of this tale and its enigmatic brevity echo a mythical tradition that is far older than its thirteenth-century transcription:

There was a city in Pouille called Sipont that had succumbed to a mighty illness. It would persist for as long as smoke emerged

---

*[The French name for this constellation translates as "the big bear." —*Trans.*]

from the mouth of Gug, who once ate forty-two (or twelve) children to cure himself of the illness afflicting his body and his soul. When the event that took place in the era of Jerusalem was 1,295 years old, the head of Gug would rot and Sipont would recover its health.

This text offers three significant mythic motifs that are worth pointing out and receiving close examination: A giant named Gug is suffering from a far from common illness; to heal himself he eats forty-two or twelve children, depending on the version of the myth; when he dies, his head is buried near Sipont.

We can no longer harbor any illusions concerning the name Gug. Near Sipont, in fact, the Mount of Gargan (which subsequently became Mont-Saint-Michel) has been known since the time of antiquity. It is clear that the true name of the giant is Gargan. Gug is merely an analogical and biblical recasting of the names Gog and Magog. Furthermore, near Sipont there is a place known as Testa de Gargano (Gargan's Head), which establishes a connection between this mountain and the sacred head of the giant. The myth inscribes the Gargantuan figure on a sacred site of paganism, thus giving it an exemplary value.

From what illness does the giant suffer? The text offers nothing specific in this regard. It is clear, however, that this illness infects the city itself. In other words, it was a calamity of mythic origin that poisoned an entire region in accordance with the principle of the shared destiny of a sovereign and his kingdom. This inevitably brings to mind the Wasteland of the Grail romances: The incurable illness of the Fisher King propagates its curse on a land that is itself stricken by every disaster.

In the Sipontine myth, the giant is obliged to sacrifice human victims in order to cure himself. This is undoubtedly the main point of this tradition. In fact, the giant Gug, like the Greek Minotaur and the Morholt from the Tristan legend, demands an actual human tribute, which makes him a sacred monster: His reappearances are likely in accord with a sacred time, or cycle, of mythic beginning during which major figures are always destined to reappear.

Accentuating the continuance of this tradition, like the Greek Chronos and the Latin Saturn, Gug-Gargan eats children. Based on this, this legend might be interpreted ritualistically: these forty-two children may represent the time the giant gives himself to survive. Symbolically, they are the forty-two days of Carnival time, which are marked by the appearance and disappearance of this god-bear, ogre, and fairy called Gargan. The numbers forty-two and twelve are explicitly allocated to a Gargantuan rite that regulates the time between the liturgies of Carnival, Mardi Gras, and Easter; Easter and the Ascension; and so forth, and which witnesses the emergence of the giant in search of his cure. No one expresses any surprise at the fact this giant eats human flesh—but that this consumption is the foundation of the major rite of Carnival does require explanation, which is precisely what we find in *The Prophecies of Merlin*. The cannibalistic feast is related to a sacred meal that takes place in a period of time that is also sacred because it provides a way of setting time.

Given these details, it is easier to grasp the religious value of the number forty within calendrical numerology. The forty martyrs of Sebasté, commemorated on March 10 in the middle of Lent or Carnival, represent the Church's need to Christianize a key figure of the pagan calendar, the true heart of the mythical mechanism of Carnival. According to legend, these forty legionnaires refused to sacrifice to pagan gods. After being tortured, they were exposed to the bitter cold of a frozen pond. Might they, then, be likened to a sacrifice offered to a kind of pagan god, much like the forty-two children that formed the repast of Gug-Gargon? Is it by chance, moreover, that a certain Gorgan is one of these forty martyrs? In this instance, Gorgon plays the role of victim, unlike Gug-Gargan, who plays the role of executioner, but here we can certainly recognize the kind of transfer that is characteristic of the Christianization process. The Church transformed the pagan myth by slightly blurring the names, yet the archaic memory remains if we restore the context of the pagan legend connected to each one of the names. Another Gorgon can be found in the company of a Saint Firme, whose feast day is March 11.

The number twelve becomes equally significant if we relate it to the context of the calendar. The Twelve Days that separate Christmas from Epiphany correspond to the time of the Saturnalia, and this period is actually a reduced image of the twelve months of the coming year. During Roman antiquity, these twelve days of the Saturnalia commemorated Saturn-Chronos, the devourer of his own children. In the Middle Ages, another massacre of children was substituted: that ordered by Herod at the time of Christ's birth.

The commemoration of the massacre of the Holy Innocents on December 28 might thus take on two meanings, depending on whether we view it from a biblical or a pagan perspective. According to the Bible, Herod slaughtered these children in the hope that he would eliminate the infant Jesus, whom he viewed as a rival (Matthew 2:13–18). In pagan tradition, the massacre of children was envisioned as a cure for diseases such as leprosy. It was believed that the illness could be banished by immersing a leper in the blood drained from healthy children. The medieval chanson de geste *Ami et Amile,* among many others, recalls this belief that also figures in the *Life of Saint Sylvester.* To cure the emperor Constantine of his leprosy, however, Saint Sylvester refused to use the blood remedy in which the emperor had placed all his faith. Instead, the saint appealed to a miracle from heaven, which subsequently compelled the emperor to convert to Christianity. It is not by chance, then, that Sylvester, celebrated on December 31, appears in the calendar at the very moment when time is about to tip and at the time of the commemoration of the Innocents, victims of an iniquitous executioner, which calls to mind the story of the saint's healing of a leprous emperor.

The thread connecting all these commemorations can be found in paganism. The basic theme at play is the healing of the giant Time, the Celtic Saturn who waits for forty days of additional life in order to open the Candlemas–Mardi Gras cycle. The testimony of a pagan tradition preserved up to the middle of the thirteenth century makes it possible to rediscover the profound consistency of a tradition that is the basis of the essential rites of the Carnival religion and which places the giant-ogre at the heart of the mystery of time.

Finally, the analogous connection that can be established between the giant Gug (or Gargan) of Mont-Saint-Michel and the Minotaur (a monster with a human body and a bull's head) can in turn explain the presence of the bull associated with the cowherd Gargan. Here we come face-to-face with two different formulations of the same Indo-European myth: Gug-Gargan is clearly the Celtic Minotaur, who is based not on the Greek Minotaur, but instead on a beast that can be traced back to a heritage shared by both the Celtic and the Hellenic peoples.

Conclusion

With regard to the subject of medieval festivals and mythology, it is important to understand that nothing has been lost or created. Instead, everything has been transformed. Of course, this is not to imply that the entire medieval festival system is necessarily explained by a network of earlier festivals. Yet a detour through Celtic traditions can findamentally renew the way we look at medieval beliefs.

All there is to be known about the genesis of the Christian calendar confirms this analytical perspective. If we recall the words of Pliny himself,[1] the Gauls used a lunar-solar calendar. The lunar month of twenty-nine and a half days was divided into two periods: The new moon signaled the beginning of the first period and the full moon heralded the second. The periodic insertion of an additional month enabled the lunar and solar cycles to catch up to one another. The old Roman calendar bore a strong resemblance to this Gallic calendar: the ides (the new moon) began the month and the calends (full moon) marked its midpoint. Julius Caesar reformed the calendar in order to avoid the periodic addition of a month, but ides and calends were retained, although they no longer corresponded to the phases of the moon.

The Christian Middle Ages inherited the Julian calendar and fixed the important commemorations primarily to the ides (from the thirteenth to the sixteenth day of the month) and to the calends (the first day of the month). Along with Christianizing key pagan figures, they shifted many of the ancient festival days to these essential dates. This explains certain intervals in the theoretical rule of the forty-day periods (corresponding to one and a half lunar month). The principle of a relative continuity between the pagan calendar and the Christian calendar of the Middle Ages is difficult to contest, for it involves the corollary examination of the myths and rites (both pagan and Christian) that are attached to this calendar.

It is true, though, that every civilization reinvents the festivals it may inherit. While an ancient tradition that we describe today as Indo-European survived into the Middle Ages, we must recognize that the medieval period proceeded to transfer, reinvent, and transform the calendrical and mythological substrata it inherited.

The Christian calendar reveals all the earlier festival elements while reconstructing them and the myths that support them. This last point is a major one: A festival is always connected to a myth; rather than being merely a celebration, it is also a commemoration. Through its rite it reactualizes the original myths that were too often neglected in the past. Moreover, it appeals to a hidden memory that the triple testimony of profane medieval literature, hagiography, and legends improperly labeled as folktales (including the medieval *exempla*) can help us to reconstruct.

Finding the trace of the authentic mythology of the Middle Ages is no easy task. To do this, we often need to resort to incomplete and heterogenous testimonies. Yet we can nonetheless begin a cross-referenced study of the rites, myths, and names relating to Carnival to reconstruct the "religious" spirit that supports these.

It therefore appears that medieval mythology is in large part a result of the folklorized form of the pagan cults that preceded Christianity. We must remember that the Christian religion was not the first Western religion and that it was introduced onto European soil at a time that is quite easy to determine. It appropriated a part of the autochthonous religion by recasting certain pagan deities and adapting them to the spirit and the letter of the evangelistic message.

At the same time, Christianity launched a studied transformation of the mythic figures of paganism. It invented new myths on top of the ancient ones. The example of Martin reveals what was lacking in this approach: The Christianization of this persona occurred as if the pagan ancestor of Saint Martin—the wild magician and the master of the flocks, life, death, and the perfect science—had to be split into two diametrically opposed figures, one luminous and sanctified (Martin), who retained his ancestor's miraculous powers (albeit now controlled by God), and a cthonian figure (the devil) who made use of a magic that was evil and destructive (or was deemed so by the Church). In numerous folktales, the devil is not based at all on a biblical model (which is almost nonexistent), but rather a mythical one that harkens back to the partially decomposed Celtic myths that were still perfectly effective in the medieval imaginal realm. For the first figure—an ambiguous magician—Christianity substituted a duality in which irreducible opposites take on the force of law. While Merlin the Wild Man was neither totally an angel nor totally a devil, Martin was forced to surrender to the horned devil a portion of his being and his powers in order to claim entry into heaven.

Today, this fact is gradually gaining recognition: Carnival belonged to the Indo-European or, to be more exact, the pre–Indo-European world and was adapted by the successive civilizations that retained it. Christianity happened to penetrate into the original religious system of the European peoples who inherited this system, a point that generally receives little emphasis in the study of the conversion of the Western world to the Christian faith. Indeed, Christianity would have had no chance of imposing itself in the West if, on certain points of dogma and rites, it had not responded to the religious needs of the converted pagans. Mysterious similarities between the Indo-European and Judeo-Christian religions enabled the latter to smoothly envelop the first.

The points of conjunction between the two belief systems merit study on their own because they are at the root of a great many methodological misunderstandings of historians. Many scholars have attributed to Christianity what rightfully belonged to the Indo-European world.

It appears today that the merger of the two worlds puts the finishing touches on a radical disruption in our understanding of the way time, death, and the sacred were conceived in later antiquity and came to govern the entire Middle Ages before slowly expiring today (or transforming yet again) before our very eyes.

History of Normandy, Book 13

From the Orderic Vital:

I do not believe I should omit or conceal the truth about what happened at the beginning of the month of January to a certain priest in the bishopric of Lisieux. Living in a village called Bonneval was a priest by the name of Gauchelin who served the church dedicated to Saint Aubin of Angers, who had gone from being a monk to being a bishop and a confessor.

In the year of our Lord 1091, at the beginning of January, this priest was summoned, quite normally, by a sick man who lived on the border of his parish. Gauchelin was returning from the patient's bedside at night. As he was walking home alone, he suddenly found himself in a spot remote from any inhabitation and he heard a noise comparable to the one a large army would make. He first thought was that it was the men of Robert de Bellême on their way to besiege Courci. The moon was then in its eighth day; it cast a very bright glow in the sign of Aries, giving those who walked an easy path.

Our priest was young, hardy, quite agile, and large in build. The noise he heard alarmed him and he considered whether he should flee to avoid being assaulted and dishonestly robbed by the odious soldiery or confront them and resist their aggression with his own strength. Some distance from the path he spotted four medlar trees standing in a field. He sought to conceal himself behind them while the cavalcade passed, but a man of huge stature armed with a club interrupted the priest's course and, raising his arm over his head, said: "Stay here and advance no farther."

Immediately, the priest came to a halt and, frozen in terror and resting on the staff he bore, remained motionless. The man armed with the club stayed close to him and, without doing him any harm, awaited the passage of the army. A large troop of phantoms began to pass, carrying over their necks and shoulders sheep, clothing, furnishings, and utensils of all kinds, like brigands have the custom of doing.

All of them were moaning and encouraging one another to double their speed. The priest recognized among them several of his neighbors who had died recently and could hear their complaints of the cruel tortures whose torments their crimes had earned them. Next, a troop of gravediggers passed by and the giant joined their company. They were laden with around fifty coffins, each of which was carried by two bearers. Sitting on these coffins were men as small as dwarves, but whose heads were the size of barrels. Two Ethiopians were charged with the trunk of an enormous tree on which a chained wretch was being cruelly tortured: His torment was causing him to utter atrocious screams. The horrible demon seated on this corpse cruelly struck it in the back and kidneys with flaming spurs, leaving it all bloody. Gauchelin had no trouble recognizing the victim: It was the murderer of the priest Etienne. He witnessed the man's horrible sufferings for the innocent blood he had spilled two years earlier and for having died without atoning for his crime.

Next, a troop of women beyond count passed before the priest's eyes. They were mounted sidesaddle on horses, and these saddles had flaming nails sticking out from them. The wind would often lift these women as high as a cubit before letting them fall back down on the nails. Because they were on fire, they burned their buttocks. Terribly tortured by both the spiking and the burning, the women screamed imprecations and publically confessed the sins that had earned them such punishment. This was why they were cruelly suffering from fire, stench, and many other tortures that do not bear retelling. They confessed, moaning in plaintive tones, about the pains they endured because of the delights and obscene pleasures to which they had devoted themselves in such excess during their lives. Our priest recognized several noble women in this troop and saw horses and mules that belonged to women who were still alive.

Seeing all this caused him to tremble and plunged him into intense reflection. Shortly thereafter, he spotted a large band of monks and clerics, with their judges and superiors, bishops and abbots holding their pastoral crosses. The clerics and bishops were clad in black copes, while the monks and abbots were wearing cowls of the same color. All were moaning and groaning; some of them even entreated Gauchelin by name and implored him, on behalf of their former friendship, to pray for them . . .

The priest continued to tremble while this dreadful procession filed before him, and, propping himself on his staff, he waited for yet more terrifying things to appear. He saw a huge army advancing; only one color could be distinguished: black interspersed with glowing flames. All those included in its mass were mounted on gigantic horses and were marching while armed to the teeth, as if rushing into battle, and they carried black banners . . .

After watching this troop of horsemen march past him, Gauchelin told himself: "These are undoubtedly Herlequin's men. I've heard say that some people have sometimes seen them but, skeptical as I was, I did not believe a word of all that because I never had real proof of its existence. But now I am truly seeing the spirits of these dead people. Yet, no one will believe me when I tell what I've seen, unless I can provide people with actual proof. I will therefore grab one of these free horses that follows these troops and mount him at once; I will ride him back home and show him to my neighbors as proof of the veracity of my story."

APPENDIX 2

The Baying (or Questing) Beast

The Quest (Demanda) for the Holy Grail,
Spanish version, chapters 357 and 358

As I am about to tell you, all three went in search of the baying beast in the direction they had seen him heading, but they did not discover him that day, no matter how fast they ran. They remained all night in the forest, though without eating or drinking because they had brought nothing with them and could find nothing there. This was how they spent the night with their horses. They resumed their ride the next day, and Galahad said to the others: "I really believe that this day will see the end of our adventure.

"Milord," the others asked, "how do you know this?"

"I have a premonition."

They pursued their way until noon. It was at this moment that they came upon the twenty dead dogs who had attacked the beast and there was great mourning and Galahad said: "My friends, the beast has passed through here; it is what slew these dogs."

While he spoke, they came across a squire who was walking on foot. They asked him if he had seen the baying beast and he answered: "Cursed be the day that I saw him, for he killed my horse and I am forced to make my way on foot."

"And which way did it go?" asked Galahad.

The squire pointed in that direction and they set off immediately.

Wending their way, they reached a valley in which lay a small and very deep lake. They spotted the beast there as it stopped to drink in order to slake its great thirst. On the shore were twenty greyhounds belonging to Palamedes. On catching sight of the beast they began barking so loud that the knights who were looking for it could hear them.

Galahad said to Perceval: "Do you hear that barking?"

"Yes," the others responded. "The beast must be down there; let's go."

Thus they hastened, and when they reached the lake they could see the beast as well as the greyhounds baying all around it. It was not so far from the shore that it was beyond reach from being struck by a lance that could easily wound it.

When they saw how things were, they approached, led by Palamedes, who was the beast's enemy because it had slain his eleven brothers and he had held a tenacious grudge against it for a long time. He drove his horse into the lake, brandishing his lance that entered one of the beast's flanks and emerged on the other side, the length of a span. The beast felt its wound and began howling so painfully that Palamedes' horse became fearful, as did the other horses, which made them difficult to restrain. Mortally wounded, the beast dove into the water and unleashed a great tempest over the lake while emitting great groans and cries. It could truly have been said that all the devils in hell were in that water. The lake began to boil and started giving off flames. Whoever witnessed it could not have helped but see it as the greatest wonder in the world. The flames did not remain for long, but the boiling water and heat lasted forever. This is why it has been named the Lake of the Baying Beast.

The three knights were quite astounded at the sight of such a marvel. When they realized that the beast would not return, Galahad said, "This beast is a great wonder. The lake has changed, for before it was cold and now it is hot. Know that it will never cease to boil."

A Short Index of Saints

This index is by no means exhaustive. It offers only a selection of saints along with the commemoration dates of saints with similar names. Only saints who lived before the twelfth century have been included.

Abondance, March 1, September 16

Abonde (Habonde), April 2, July 11, February 27, April 14, September 16

Abundius, August 26; December 10, 14

Acaclus, March 10, 31; July 28; April 28; November 27

Acepsimas, April 22, November 3

Acharius, November 27

Achille, May 15

Achillée, January 17, April 23, May 12

Achius and Acheolus, May 1

Acyndius, April 20 and November 2

Adalbert, April 22; June 20, 25

Adalgis, June 2

Adalsindis, December 25

Adaltrude, November 14

Adelard, January 2

Adelphus, August 29, September 11

Adolf, February 11

Agape, January 25; February 15; March 24; April 28, 29; August 4; November 2; December 28

Agatha, February 5

Aichard, September 15

Aigulf, May 22, September 3

Alan, November 25, December 27

Alban, June 21, 22

Alberic, July 21; August 21, 29

Alburga, December 25

Alexis, July 17

Amand, February 6; April 6; June 16, 18, 25; October 16, 26; November 13

Ambroise, August 16, 28; September 3; October 16; December 7

Anastasia, March 10, April 15, October 28, December 25

Andrew, November 30

Anicet, April 17, July 10, August 12

Anthony the Abbot (Anthony of
    Egypt), January 17

Apollinaris, January 5; February 9;
    June 21; July 23; August 23;
    September 12; October 5, 6;
    November 27

Archelaus, August 23

Arigius, May 1

Arnulf, January 29; July 18, 24;
    August 15; September 19;
    October 31

Artaldus (Arthaud), October 6

Artemius, April 28

Arthelais, January 24, March 3

Athanasius, January 3, July 5,
    November 1

Attila, October 5

Aurelia, September 25; October 14,
    15

Aurelien, May 8, June 16, July 4

Austreberta (Eustreberta),
    February 10

Austremonius, November 1

Aventinus, February 4, June 13

Avertin (a form of Aberdeen, also
    known as Aventinius), May 5

Bagnus (Bain), June 20

Baiulus, December 20

Baius, October 30

Balai, July 12

Balin, September 3

Barbara, December 4

Bartholomew, August 24

Basil, January 1; February 27;
    March 4, 6, 22, 26; April 12;
    June 14; July 9; October 29

Benigne, November 1

Bernard of Clairvaux, August 20

Bertha, May 1

Bertillia, January 3

Blaesilla, January 22

Blain, August 10

Blaise, February 3

Brendan, May 16, November 29

Brigid, February 1

Britte, January 15

Bruno, October 6

Cadoc, January 24

Caesarius, February 25; April 20;
    August 27; November 1, 3;
    December 28

Calliope, April 7, June 8

Caradoc, April 13

Carantog, November 16

Carpophorus, April 7, 27; August 20;
    November 8; December 10

Castor, February 13, April 27,
    September 21, December 28

Catherine, November 25

Christopher, July 25

Clement, November 23

Colomban, February 15,
    November 21

Corentin, December 12

Corneilius, February 2, March 31,
    June 2, September 16

Crispin and Crispinian, October 25

Cucuphas (Cucufate, Cugat), July 25

Irene, February 21, 26; April 3, 16; July 28; October 20

Isaurus, June 17

Isberga, May 21

Isidore, January 2, February 5, April 17, May 15, August 4, November 4

Ivi, October 6

Jacut, February 8

James the Greater, July 25

James the Lesser, May 1

Januarius, January 7, 19; April 8; July 10, 15; September 19; October 13, 25; December 2, 15

John the Apostle, December 27

John the Baptist, June 24

Jerome, September 30

Jovinian, May 5

Jovinus, March 2, 26

Jules, May 27, June 2, July 1, December 20

Julia, April 16; May 22; June 2; July 15, 27

Julian, January 7, 9, 27; February 12, 19, 24, 27; March 16, 23

Just (Justa), February 25, 28; May 28; June 17; July 14, 21; October 14, 18; November 2, 26; December 14

Justina, January 10, May 14, June 16, October 7, November 30

Juvenal, May 3, 7

Juventius, January 23, June 1, October 28

Juvin, October 3

Ké, October 7

Kentingern, January 13

Kevin, June 3

Kilian, July 8, November 13

Kinneburga (Cyneburgh), March 6

Kinneswith (Cyneswith), March 6

Kycarion, June 7

Laetus, November 5

Lambert, April 14, 16; September 17; October 9

Landulphus, August 18, January 19

Latuin, June 2

Laura, August 18, October 19

Lawrence, August 10

Lazarus, December 17

Leo, January 22; March 1, 14; June 30

Leonard, November 6

Leothade and Leothadius, October 23

Leucius, January 11, 28

Libaire, October 8

Livier, July 17

Lo, September 22

Longinius, March 15, April 24, May 2, June 24, July 21

Louis, August 25

Lucian, January 7, 8; May 28; June 13; July 7; November 4; December 24

Lucy, June 25, July 6, September 19, November 7, December 13

Luke, October 18

Lupercus, October 3

Luperculus, April 1

Lupicinius, February 3, March 21, May 31, June 24, December 14

Lupus, January 27; May 22; July 29; September 1, 25; October 14, 17, 19, 25; December 2

Lydia, March 27, August 3

Macarius, January 2, 15; February 6, 28; April 1

Maccabees, August 1

Malo, November 15

Malulf, May 4

Mamertius, May 11

Mappalicus, February 21, April 17

Marcel, January 16, November 1

Marculf (Marcoul), May 1

Marguerite, July 20

Mark, April 25

Martha, July 29

Martial, June 30, October 13

Martin, February 28; March 20; June 21, 23; July 1, 19; October 24; November 26

Martin of Tours, November 11

Martinian, January 3; February 13; July 2, 27

Mathan, November 14

Mathurin, November 1

Matthew, September 21

Maur, January 15, 20, 29; July 27; August 1, 22; November 21; December 3, 4, 10

Maxentius, April 30, November 20, December 12

Maxima, September 2, October 16, November 26

Melasippus, January 17

Menehould, October 14

Menna, October 3

Mercurius, November 25, December 10

Meriadoc, June 7

Merry, August 29

Metrophanes, June 4

Michael (the Archangel), May 8 (his feast day) and September 29 (commemorates his appearance at his sanctuary at Monte Gargano)

Milon, February 23, August 18

Mitrius, November 13

Modestus, January 12; February 12, 24; March 13; June 15; October 2; November 4, 10

Mommelin, October 16

Monica, May 4

Montanus, February 24, March 26, June 17, September 20, November 14

Munessa, November 14

Myron, August 3, 17

Nabor, June 12; July 10, 12

Narcissus, January 2; March 18; September 17; October 29, 31

Nectarius, August 1, September 13, December 9

Neomadius, January 14

Neon, April 24, 28; August 23; September 28; December 2

Nepotian, October 22

Nereus, May 12, October 16

Perpetua, March 7, April 8,
October 4

Peter, June 29, August 1

Petroc, June 4

Petronilla, May 31, June 6

Petronius, January 10, September 6,
October 4

Phalier, November 23

Pharaildis, January 4

Pharmuthe, April 11

Pharnacius, June 24

Phebade, April 25

Philadelphius, May 10, September 2

Philappian, January 30

Philaster, July 18

Phileas, February 4, November 26

Philemon, March 8, 21;
November 22

Philip, May 1

Philoctimon, March 10

Philogonius, December 20

Philomenas, July 5, August 10,
November 29

Phocas, March 5, July 14,
September 22

Photina, March 20

Pipe, October 7

Pirman, November 3

Placid, October 5, 11

Plato, April 4, July 22

Polueuctus, February 13, May 21

Polycarp, January 26, February 23,
April 2

Polychronius, February 17, 23

Pontian, January 19; August 25;
December 2, 11

Porcarius, August 12, October 8

Porcharius, June 1

Porphyrius, February 10, 16, 26;
September 6; November 4

Potamon, May 18

Potentian, December 31

Pothinus, June 2

Precord, February 1

Primitiva, April 16, June 10, July 18

Primus, January 3, February 9,
October 7

Priscian, September 16; October 12,
14

Priscus, March 10, 28; May 9;
June 13; September 16

Privat, September 20, 28; August 21

Prix, January 25, May 26

Probus, January 12, March 15

Procopius, February 27; July 4, 8;
November 4

Protasius, November 24

Prudentius, April 6, 28; May 6

Publius, January 21, 25; April 16;
November 2, 12

Pyrrhus, November 4

Quadratus, May 7, 26; August 21

Quartus, May 10, December 18

Quenburga, August 31

Quentin, October 31

Quinctilius, March 8, 19

Quinctus, January 4,
March 19

Quintus, March 2, May 10

Quirinus, March 25, 30; June 4;
October 11

Quiteria, May 22

Quodvultus, February 19

Radegund, August 13

Ragenufle, July 14

Ralph, June 21

Ramirus, March 11

Raphael, October 24

Redemptus, Aptil 8

Regina, September 7

Regulus, March 30, September 3

Remigius, October 10

Richimir, January 17

Rictiovarus, July 6

Rigomer, August 24

Riquier (Richarius), April 26

Rogatian, May 24, December 28

Romanus, February 9, 28; April 13;
    May 22; August 9, 24; October
    6; November 7, 18, 24

Romphaire (Romicer), November 26

Romulus, February 17, March 24,
    July 6, August 21, September 5

Rouin, February 17, March 24

Rufinus, February 27; April 7;
    August 11, 19, 26;
    September 9

Rufus, August 27; September 25;
    November 1, 7, 12

Rusticus, April 25; August 9, 17, 18;
    September 24; October 9, 14, 26;
    December 31

Rutilius, June 4, August 2

Sabina, August 29, October 27

Sabinian, January 29; June 7;
    September 25; November 1, 22

Sabinus, January 17, February 9,
    March 13, July 20, October 15,
    December 30

Salarius, October 22

Salvinus, September 4, 10;
    October 12, 28

Sature, March 29

Saturnius, January 19, 31; February
    11, 15, 21; March 7, 22;
    April 7, 16; May 2; August
    22; October 6, 14, 16, 21, 30;
    November 15, 27, 29;
    December 15, 23, 29

Satyrus, January 12, June 25,
    August 19, September 17

Savina, January 30, July 11,
    October 9

Scariberge, October 2

Sebastian, January 20

Seleucus, February 16, March 24

Septimus, September 22,
    October 24

Sergius, February 24, July 27,
    December 17

Servatus, May 13

Severus, February 1, October 1,
    November 1

Sidoine, August 21

Siegfried, February 15, August 22

Solina, October 17

Solomon, June 25

Speusippas, January 17

Spyridon, December 14

Styriacus, November 2

Superius, June 26

Syagrius, August 27

Sylvanus, February 6, 10, 18, 20;
    March 8; May 4, 5, 24; July 10,
    30; September 4, 22; October 16;
    December 2
Sylvester, March 10, May 10,
    November 20, December 31
Symphorian, July 7, August 22
Symphorosa, July 2, 18
Syrus, August 3, December 9

Tanguy, November 18
Tatian, March 16, September 12
Taurinus, September 5, August 11
Taurion, November 7
Teilo, February 9, November 25
Tetricus, March 18
Thais, October 8
Theodoric (Thierry), July 1,
    August 5
Thomas, December 21
Thyrsus, January 24, 28, 31;
    September 24
Triverius, January 16
Tropez, April 29, May 17
Trophimus, March 11, 18; July 23;
    September 19; December 29
Tryphon, April 19, July 3,
    November 10
Turpin, July 26
Tyrannio, February 20

Ulphe, January 31
Ulpian, April 3
Ulpius, June 2
Urbitius, March 20, June 3
Urciscenus, June 21

Ursanne, July 24
Ursicinus, June 19; July 24;
    August 14; October 2;
    December 1, 13, 20
Ursinus, November 9
Ursion, September 29
Ursmar, April 19
Ursula, October 21
Ursus, February 1; April 13; July 27,
    30; September 30

Valentine, January 7; February
    14; March 16; May 2; July 4,
    16; August 20; September 2;
    October 25; November 3, 11, 13;
    December 16
Vedast, February 6
Vincent, January 22
Vital, January 11; March 9;
    April 21, 28; June 2; July 2;
    September 22; October 16;
    November 3, 4
Vivian, August 28
Vulflagius (Wulphy, Vulphy), June 7
Vulganius, November 3
Vulmar, July 20

Walburga, February 25
Walfrid, February 15, October 21
Wandrille, July 22
Waudru, April 9
Werburga, February 3
Wiborada, May 2
Wilfetrudis, November 23
Wilgefortis, July 20
William of Gellone, May 28

Notes

INTRODUCTION

1. *Sancti Gregorii magni registrum epitularum,* Turnot 1982 *(Corpus Christiano-rum, series latina,* CXLA). See also *Dictionnaire d'archéologie chrétienne et de liturgie,* "Paganism."
2. From Bede, *History of the English Church and People.*
3. *Le Carnival* (Paris: Payot, 1974), 18.
4. His *Otia Imperialia* (Imperial Recreations) constitutes a veritable treasury of medieval folklore. See A. Duchesne's translation published under the title *Le livre des Merveilles* (Paris: Belles Lettres, 1992).
5. C. Hefele, *Histoire des counciles d'après les documents originaux,* vol. 3, French translation of the second German edition of 1873–82 (Paris: n.p., 1907), 837–43.
6. *L'Artiste,* February 8, 1845. Text reprinted in *En marge des Illuminés,* edited by Lemaître (Paris: Garnier, 1966), 384–87.
7. C. Vogel, *Le Pécheur et la pénitence au moyen age* (Paris: Le Cerf, 1969), 101.
8. *Patrologie latine* 89, 1036–50; U. Engelmann, *Der hl. Pirmin und sein Mission-buchlein* (Constance, 1959).
9. Mircea Eliade, *Méphistophélès et l'Androgyne* (Paris: Gallimard, 1962), 163.
10. Georges Dumézil, *Fêtes romanes d'été et d'automne* (Paris: Gallimard, 1975); on the Volcanalia, 61.
11. Philippe Walter, *La Mémoire du temps: Fêtes et calendriers de Chrétien de Troyes à La Mort Artu* (Paris: Champion, 1989).
12. In *A Plus Haut Sens,* 2 volumes (Paris: Maisonneuve et Larose, 1986).

CHAPTER 1: CARNIVAL, THE ENIGMA OF A NAME

1. See P. Zumthor, *Langue, texte, énigme* (Paris: Le Seuil, 1975), 144–60.
2. Isidorus Hispalensis, *Etymologiae* (Paris: n.p., 1981), Book 1, 24.

3. C. Baroja, *Le Carnival* (Madrid: n.p., 1965); A. van Gennep, *Manuel de folklore français contemporain* (Paris: Picard, 1947). Republished under the title *Le Folklore français* (Paris: R. Laffont, 1998–1999), 1–3, 872 ff.
4. Ovid, *Fasti,* translated by A. J. Boyle and R. D. Woodard (London: Penguin, 2000), Book 6, 129 ff.
5. The best mythological dossier on Carna can be found in Georges Dumézil's *Idées romaines* (Paris: Gallimard, 1969), 253–71.
6. Text cited after the article by Georges Dumézil.
7. C. Baroja, *Le Carnival,* 22–23.
8. Georges Dumézil, *Fêtes romaines d'été et d'automne,* 225–31.
9. The romance was published in 1884 by H. Suchier (Paris: Société des anciens textes français). It was translated into modern French by C. Marchello Nizia in 1980 (Collection Stock plus, Middle Ages).
10. *Revue de l'histoire des religions* 10 (1884), 193–209; 13 (1886), 83–96 and 215–18; and 14 (1886), 228–32.
11. Claude Lecouteux, *Mélusine ou le Chevalier au cygne* (Paris: Payot, 1982).

CHAPTER 2: NOVEMBER 1, SAMHAIN

1. F. Le Roux, "Le calendrier gaulois de Coligny et la fête irlandaise de Samain," in *Ogam* 9 (1957), 337–42. F. Le Roux and C. Guyonvarc'h, *Les Fêtes celtiques* (Rennes: Ouest-France, 1995), 35–82 and 183–86.
2. "La maladie de Cuchulainn," translation and commentary by C. Guyonvarc'h, *Ogam* 10 (1958), 285–310.
3. O. Jodogne, "L'Autre Monde celtique dans la literature française au XII siècle," in *Bulletin de l'Académie royale de Belgique,* 5th series, vol. 1, no. 46 (1960), 548–97.
4. In 1892, J. G. Bulliot and F. Thiollier published *La Mission et le culte de saint Martin d'après les legends et les monuments populaires dans les pays éduen* (Autun). They presented this work as a "study of rural paganism."
5. For more on the folk version of Saint Martin, see the investigations of Henri Fromage in *Bulletin de la Société de mythologie française* 74 (1969), 74–84 and 93–102; 78 (1970), 83–106; 83 (1971), 164, 175; and 108 (1978), 1–28.
6. *De miraculis S. Martini,* chapter 31 (see *Dictionnaire d'archéologie chrétienne et de liturgie,* "Paganism," chapter 30).
7. M. Praneuf, *L'Ours et les hommes dans les traditions européennes* (Paris: Imago, 1989).
8. R. Bernheimer, *Wild Men in the Middle Ages* (Cambridge: n.p., 1952).
9. H. Rey-Flaud, *Le Charivari* (Paris: Payot, 1985), 120–22.
10. [Translated by W. W. Comfort (London: Everyman's Library, 1914).—*Trans.*]

11. P. Zumthor, *Merlin le Prophète* (Lausanne: 1943; reprinted Geneva: Slatkine, 2000).

12. [Translated by Alexander Roberts (New York, n.p., 1894).—*Trans.*]

13. P. Walter, *Merlin ou le Savoir du monde* (Paris: Imago, 2000).

14. *Pantagruel,* translated by J. M. Cohen (London: Penguin, 1955), Book 2, chapter 28, 258.

15. H. Gaidoz, *Saint Hubert et la Rage* (Paris: Picard, 1887); B. Hell, *Le Sang noir: Chasse et mythe du Sauvage en Europe* (Paris: Gallimard, 1994).

16. Marie de France, *Lais,* new edition and translation by Philippe Walter (Paris: Gallimard, 2000).

17. During the Middle Ages, it was the legend of Saint Eustache (October 12) that contained the lion's share of the themes of the legends concerning Saint Hubert. See A. Boureau, *L'Événement sans fin* (Paris: Les Belles Lettres, 1993), 83–135.

CHAPTER 3: CHRISTMAS AND THE TWELVE DAYS

1. Claude Lecouteux, "Le repas des fees," in *Bulletin du Comité du folklore champenois* 149 (1988), 49; and 150 (1988), 3–9.

2. Extract from the *Otia imperialia,* quoted from the translation by Claude Lecouteux in the above-mentioned article.

3. From A. Maury's translation (Paris: Gallimard, 1949), 310.

4. A. Maury, *Les Fées au Moyen Age* (Paris: Champion, 1896), 21.

5. A translation of this text is included as appendix 1 of this book.

6. See various articles from the *Revue des Traditions populaires* 9 (1894), 411–14; 13 (1898), 451–55; 16 (1901), 531; 17 (1902), 504–05.

7. R. Fawtier, *La Vie de saint Samson: Essai critique hagiographique* (Paris: Champion, 1912).

8. *Le Problème des Centaures* (Paris: Geuthner, 1929), 15.

9. All the useful references can be found in Philippe Walter, "Der Bar und der Erzbischof: Masken und Mummentanz bei Hinkmar von Reims und Adalbero von Laon," in *Feste und Feiern im Mittelalter, Sigmaringen* (1991), 377–88.

10. M. Eliade, *Forgerons et Alchimistes* (Paris: Flammarion, 1977), 90–91.

11. Ibid., 88.

12. Tobler-Lommatzch, *Altfranzösisches Wörterbuch* (Wiesbaden: Steiner, 1925), under "mire," vol. 6, 75.

13. See the Du Cange Dictionary, in which the expression *digitus medicinalis* is mentioned as occurring in Book 7, chapter 13, of the *Saturnalias* by Macrobius.

14. Claus is a deformation of Niklaus and Nicholas.

CHAPTER 4: FEBRUARY 1, IMBOLC

1. F. Le Roux and C. Guyonvarc'h, *Les Fêtes celtiques,* 83–97 and 187–200.

2. P. G. d'Ayala and M. Boiteux, *Carnavals et Mascarades* (Paris: Bordas, 1988).

3. *Französisches Etymologisches Wörterbuch* (Tübingen: Mohr, 1948), 429–41.

4. J. P. Migne, *Patrologie latine,* vol. 125 (Paris, n. p., 1844–64).

5. A. van Gennep, "Manuel de folklore français contemporain," in *Tome* 1, no. 3, 1078.

6. For more on the connection between masks and revenants in the Middle Ages, see J. C. Schmitt, "Les Masques, le diable, les morts dans l'Occident medieval," in *Razo* 6 (1986), 87–119.

7. C. Lecouteux, "Mara, ephialtes, incubus," in *Etudes germaniques* 42 (1987), 1–24.

8. L. Knappert, "La Vie de saint Gall et le pagnisme germanique," in *Revue de l'histoire des religions* 29 (1984), 259–95.

9. Aymon de Varennes, *Florimont,* edited by A. Hilke (Göttingen: n.p., 1932).

10. W. Stoke, "The Boccan's Hymn," in *Thesaurus Paleohibernicus,* vol. 2 (Cambridge: n.p., 1903), 343 ff.

11. I. Grange, "Métamorphoses chrétiennes des femmes-cygnes: du folklore à l'hagiographie," in *Ethnologie française* 13 (1983), 130–50.

12. Claude Lecouteux, *Fées, sorcières et loups-garous* (Paris: Imago, 1992), 68–69. English edition: *Witches, Werewolves, and Fairies* (Rochester, Vt: Inner Traditions, 2004), 54–55.

13. C. Guyonvarc'h and F. Le Roux, *Morrigan, Bodb, Macha, la souveraineté guerrière de l'Irlande* (Rennes: Editions Ouest, 1983).

14. Bertrand de Marseille, *La Vie de sainte Enimie,* edited by C. Brunel (Paris: n.p., 1917).

15. This text dates from 881. It was edited by R. L. Wagner, *Textes d'étude* (Geneva and Paris: n.p., 1949).

16. Book 5, chapter 4.

17. C. Gaignebet, *A Plus Haut Sens.*

18. C. Guyonvarc'h and F. Le Roux, *Morrigan, Bodb, Macha, la souveraineté guerrière de l'Irlande.*

19. A. H. Knappe, "Les Dieux au courbeau chez les Celtes," in *Revue de l'histoire des religions* 114 (1936), 236–46.

20. Giraut de Barri, *Topographica hibernica* (Topography of Ireland), vol. 5, edited by J. F. Dimrock (London: n.p., 1867), 114.

21. J. Leroy, *Sainte Marie de Boulogne* (Montreuil-sur-Mer: n.p., 1985).

22. C. Lecouteux, *Mélusine et le chevalier au cygne.*

23. B. Cousée, *Le Coq: Folklore et mythologie d'un oiseau* (Lille: self-published, 1992).

24. C. Gaignebet, "Sur le Jeudi-jeudiot," in *Bulletin folklorique de l'Ile-de-France* 8 (1968), 35–44.

25. J. M. Bovin, *L'Irlande au Moyen Age: Giraut de Barri et la topographia hibernica* (Paris: Champion, 1993), 211–15).

26. C. Fabre-Vassas, *La Bête singulière: Les juifs, les chrétiens et le cochon* (Paris: Gallimard, 1994).

27. P. Walters, ed., *Mythologie du porc* (Grenoble: Millon, 1999).

28. The case of Anthony is not isolated. See C. Méchin, "Les Saints gardiens de pourceux," in *Revue des sciences socials de la France de l'Est* 9 (1980), 286–92 and 10 (148–63).

29. P. Walter, ed., *Saint Antoine entre mythe et légende* (Grenoble: Ellug, n.d.).

CHAPTER 5: THE TRANSITIONAL PERIOD OF EASTER

1. G. Dumézil, *Le Festin d'immortalité* (Paris: Geuthner, 1924), 237.

2. R. S. Loomis, *The Grail: From Celtic Myth to Christian Symbol* (New York, n.p., 1963); P. Walters, *La Mémoire du temps: Fêtes et calendriers de Chrétien de Troyes à la Mort Arthu* (Paris: Champion, 1989), 319–26 and 509–21.

3. C. Vogel, "Pratiques superstitieuses au début du XI siècle d'après le *Corrector sive medicus* de Burchard, évêque de Worms (965–1025)," in *Mélanges E. R. Labande* (Paris: Poitiers, 1974), 754.

4. C. Lecouteux, *Witches, Werewolves, and Fairies.*

5. R. Mathieu, "Le Lièvre de la lune dans l'antiquité chinoise," in *Revue de l'histoire des religions* 207 (1990), 339–65.

6. Claude Lévi-Strauss, *Mythologiques 2: Du miel aux cendres* (Paris: Plon, 1967), 350.

7. S. Czarnowski, *Le Culte des héros et ses conditions socials: Saint Patrick, héro national de l'Irlande* (Paris: Alcan, 1919).

8. On this tradition, see P. Bonnechere, "La Personnalité mythologique de Trophonios," in *Revue de l'histoire des religions* 216 (1999), 259–97.

9. J. Le Goff, *La Naissance du Purgatoire* (Paris: Gallimard, 1981).

10. P. Brunel, *L'Evocation des morts et la descente aux enfers: Homère, Virgile, Dante, Claudel* (Paris: Sedes, 1974).

11. *La vie de saint Bénézet,* Provençal text from the thirteenth century, edited by Abbé J. H. Albanès (Marseilles: Camoin, 1876). See also Vincent de Beauvais, *Speculum historiale,* Book 29, chapter 21.

12. G. Widengren, "Le Légende royale de l'Iran antique," in *Latomos* (Mélanges Dumézil) 45 (1960), 225–37.

13. P. Sébillot, *Gargantua dans les traditions populaires* (Paris: Maisonneuve et Larose, 1853).

14. F. Delpech, "Rite, légende, mythe et société: Fondations et fondateurs dans la tradition folklorique de la peninsula ibérique," in *Medieval Folklore* 1 (1991), 10–56.

15. Ibid., 20–21.

16. G. Dumézil, *Du Mythe au roman* (Paris: PUF, 1983), 183.

17. E. Löseth, *Le Roman en prose de Tristan: Analyse critique* (Paris: n.p., 1981), 81.

18. C. Cahier, *Characteristiques des saints dans l'art populaire* (Paris: Poussielgue Frères, 1867).

19. P. Sébillot, *Le Folklore de France,* vol. 7: *Les Monuments* (Paris: Imago, 1985), 132–33.

20. In Artois, see Ternick, *Promenades sur la chaussée Brunehaut* (1841). See also J. Vannérus, *La Reine Brunehaut dans la toponymie et dans la légende* (Brussels: Royal Academy of Belgium, 1938).

21. M. Sahlin, *Étude sur la carole médievale: L'origine du mot et ses rapports avec l'Eglise* (Uppsala: Almquist and Wiksells, 1940).

22. P. Verrier, "La Plus Veille Citation de carole," in *Romania* 58 (1932), 380–421.

23. Another French folk song mentions a dance on a bridge: "Su'l pont du Nord / Un bal y est donné . . ." [On North Bridge / A ball is given. —*Trans.*].

24. P. Saintyves, "Le theme des pierres qui boivent ou se baignent," in *Revue de folklore française* 5 (1934), 213–16.

CHAPTER 6: MAY 1, BELTANE

1. M. F. Gueusquin, *Le Mois des dragons* (Paris: Berger-Levrault, 1981).

2. F. Le Roux and C. Guyonvarc'h, *Les Fêtes celtiques* (Rennes: Editions Ouest-France, 1995), 99–111 and 201–202.

3. Lefèvre de Saint-Rémy, *Chronique* of 1408–1436 (Paris: F. Morand, 1876–81. The part of 1408–1423 was published by Le Laboureur, *Le Religieux de saint Denis,* vol. 1, 1–167, and Buchon, *Collection des chroniques,* vols. 32–33.

4. C. Vogel, "Pratiques superstitieuses au début du XI siècle d'après le *Corrector sive Medicus* de Burchard, évêque de Worms (965–1025)," in *Mélanges E. R. Labande,* 759.

5. Translation from the text provided by the *Chrestomathie provençale* by Bartsch (1904), 121–22.

6. C. Guyonvarc'h, *Textes mythologiques irlandais,* vol. 1 (Rennes: Editions Ouest-France, 1980).

7. *Otia imperialia,* Book 3, 86.

8. *Tristan et Iseut: Les texts français,* edited and translated by Philippe Walter (Paris: Le Livre de Poche, 1989), 66, verses 948–54.

9. Cited by A. van Gennep, *Manuel de folklore français contemporain,* vols. 1–4, 1455.

10. Georges Dumézil, "Temps et mythes," in *Recherches philosophiques* 5 (1935), 235–51.

11. This text was translated by R. Roth, *Indische Studien,* vol. 1, 457–64; vol. 2, 111–28.

12. For more on this mythic figure, see J. M. Privat, ed., *Dans la Gueule du dragon* (Sarreguemines: Pierron, 2000).

CHAPTER 7: SAINT JOHN'S DAY

1. C. Lecouteux, *Witches, Werewolves, and Fairies.*

2. Julius Caesar, *The Gallic Wars,* Book 6, chapter 14.

3. D. Fabre, *Jean de l'Ours, analyse formelle et thématique d'un conte populaire* (Carcassonne, n.p., 1969). See also by the same author "L'Ours ravissuer dans les *Mirabilia et les Histoires naturelles,*" in *Via Domitia* 6 (1970), 51–72.

4. G. Guenin, "Le Culte des pierres en Gaule et en France d'après les texts contemporains du Vieme au xieme siècle," in *Revue de folklore français* 3 (1932), 97–105.

5. A. Audin, "Les Rites solsticiaux et la légende de saint Pothin," in *Revue de l'histoire des religions* 96 (1927), 147–74.

6. J. Gricourt, "Un mell benniget gaelique," in *Ogam* 7 (1955), 155–70.

7. P. Walter, *Le Gant de verre: Le mythe de Tristan et Yseult* (La Gacilly: Ed. Artus, 1990), 123–52.

8. C. Vogel, "Pratiques superstieuses au début de XI siècle d'après le *Corrector sive medicus* de Burchard, évêque de Worms (965–1025)," in *Mélanges E. R. Labande,* 753.

9. Text translated after verses 679–770 from the interpolation of A. Langfor's manuscript E.

10. L. Galactéros de Boissier and Y. Giraud, "Fortune et sa roué dans le Jeu de la Feuillée," in *L'Information littéraire* 34 (1982), 54–60.

CHAPTER 8: AUGUST 1, LUGHNASA

1. F. Le Roux and C. Guyonvarc'h, *Les Fêtes celtiques,* 113–63 and 203–211.

2. See appendix 2 at the end of this book.

3. L. Dumont, *La Tarasque* (Paris: Gallimard, 1951).

4. The text of this legend consigned by P. Pons was published in *Le Monde alpin et rhodanian* 2 (1973), 70.

5. M. Eliade, *Aspects du mythe* (Paris: Gallimard, 1963), 72.

6. G. Dumézil, *Myth et Épopée*, vol. 3 (Paris: Gallimard, 1973); *Fêtes romaines d'été et d'automne* (Paris: Gallimard, 1975): the *Neptunalia* (25–31) and the *Furrinalia* (32–37). The quote from Dionysius of Halicarnassus (12, 11) is examined on 63 ff. of *Myth et épopée,* vol 3.

7. G. Paris, *Les Danseurs maudits: Légende allemande du XIe siècle* (Paris: Bouillon, 1900).

8. B. Robreau, *Les Miracles de Notre Dame de Chartres: Recherches sur la structure* (Chartres: Archaeological Society of Eure-et-Loir, 1994).

9. P. Sébillot, *Le Folklore de France*, vol. 4 (1904–06). Reprint (Paris: Imago, 1983), 227.

10. H. Dontenville, *Mythologie française* (Paris: Payot, 1948). Reprinted 1973, 46.

11. *Homilia de sacrilegiis,* chapter 3. Caspari edition cited in D. Harmening, *Superstitio* (Berlin: n.p., 1979), 54 and 147.

12. Gerhardt, *Old Men of the Sea from Neptunus to Old French "Luiton"* (Utrecht: n.p., 1967), and P. Walter, *Canicule: Essai de mythologie sur Yvain de Chrétien de Troyes* (Paris: Sedes, 1988), 141–53.

13. Chaillan, *Les Saintes Maries de la mer* (Marseilles: n.p., 1926), with documents on the fifteenth-century excavations; P. Amargier, *Les Saintes Maries de la mer au Moyen Age* (Aix-en-Provence: n.p., 1985); J. Chocheyras, *Les Saintes de la mer* (Orléans: Paradigme, 1995).

14. J. Chocheyras, *Les Saintes de la mer,* 127–36.

15. *Les villes mortes du golfe de Lyon* (Paris: Plon, 1883), 416–17.

16. For more on the archaeological proof of these cults to the mother goddesses in the regions related to the saints of the sea, see J. Chocheyras, *Les Saintes de la mer,* 37–41.

17. D. Poirion, "Le role de la fée Morgue et de ses compagnes dans le *Jeu de la Feuillée,"* in *Bulletine bibliographique de la Société internationale arthurienne* 18 (1966), 125–35.

18. A. Maury, *Croyances et légendes du Moyen Age* (Paris: n.p., 1896), 23.

19. C. Lecouteux, "Les cynocéphales," in *Cahiers de civilization médiévale* 24 (1981), 117–28.

20. J.-C. Schmitt, *Le Saint lévrier: Guignefort guérissuer d'enfants depuis le XIIIe siècle* (Paris: Flammarion, 1979).

CHAPTER 9: SAINT MICHAEL ON MOUNT GARGAN

1. *Revue des traditions populaires* (1900), 465–67.

2. *Patrologie latine,* 94, col. 502: *In revelationem s. Michaelis.*

3. *Patrologie latine,* 135, col. 853: *De triumphis Christi apud Italiam.*

4. Cited, ed., *Tristan et Iseut,* 148–49, v. 2733.

5. Ibid., 632–33.

6. J. E. Drochon, *Histoire illustrée des pèlerinages français de la très sainte Vierge Marie* (Paris: Plon, 1890), 775.

7. A. Prost, "La Colonne de Merten et le monument de Seltz," in *Bulletin de la Société nationale des Antiquaires de France* (1879), 68–85; and "Les Travaux consacrés au groupe de l'anguipède et du cavalier jusqu'en 1891," in *Mémoires de la Société nationale des Antiquaires de France* 52 (1892), 1–42.

8. G. Henderson, "The Feast of Bricriu," in *Irish Texts Society* 2 (1899).

9. A. Reinach, "Le Rite des têtes coupées chez les celtes," in *Revue de l'histoire des religions* 67 (1913), 41–48; and "Les Têtes coupées et les trophées en Gaule," in *Revue celtique* 34 (1913), 38–60 and 253–86. P. Lambrechts, *L'Exaltation de la tête dans la pensée et dans l'art des celtes* (Bruges: De Tempel, 1954).

10. B. Krusch, ed., "Gesta Dagoberti Regis Francorum," in *Monumenta Germaniae Historica, Scriptores,* vol. 2, 399–425.

11. C. Gaignebet, "L'Homme qui a vu l'homme, qui a vu l'homme, qui a vu . . . ," in *Poétique* 45 (1981), 1–8.

12. Guiges le Chartreux, *Vie de Saint Hugues, éveque de Grenoble,* translated by M. A. Chomel (Grenoble: Ed. Des Cahiers de l'Alpe, 1984).

13. *Notice archéologique sur le département de l'Oise* (Beauvais, 1856).

14. L. A. Paton, ed., *Les Propheties de Merlin,* ms. 591 of the Rennes Municipal Library (New York and London: n.p., 1926–27).

CONCLUSION

1. P. M. Duval, "Les Gaulois et le calendrier," in *Mélanges Carcopino* (Paris: Hachette, 1966), 295–311. E. Linckenheld, "Pline et le calendrier gaulois," *Revue celtique* 48 (1931), 137–44.

Index

Page numbers in italics refer to illustrations